When the Road is

ROUGH AND STEEP

To Tom and Beverly

May the Lord continue to pour
down blessings upon you, your
family and your ministry.

Your friend in Jesus

Harry.

Ps. 126: 5-6.

When the Road is

ROUGH AND STEEP

MESSAGES FROM THE BIBLE FOR THOSE FACING HARDSHIPS

Tragedy

Hardship

Depression

Doubt

Anguish

Cost

HARRY KILBRIDE

Pleasant Word

Pleasant Word (a division of WinePress Publishing, PO Box 428, Enumclaw, WA 98022) functions only as book publisher. As such, the ultimate design, content, editorial accuracy, and views expressed or implied in this work are those of the author.

ISBN 1-4141-0513-4
Library of Congress Catalog Card Number: 2005905976

For June

Contents

Introduction

Some who come to faith in Christ are given the idea that life will now be a bed of roses. They soon find it otherwise. Tragedies, trials, and tears are often the lot of both Christian and non-Christian alike. Where is God at such times and why does he allow his children such suffering? That is what this book is about.

I have been a preacher of the Gospel for fifty years. Of the many hundreds of sermons I have preached over that time, some of the most appreciated have been those dealing with hardships and sorrow. This book is a compilation of some of them.

The sermons are, of course, based upon the Bible, which is God's Word. If there are answers to be had, it is in the Bible that they will be found. God is not obligated to answer all our questions nor does he need to explain himself. But sometimes he does.

The first chapter, entitled "Tragedy," describes a horrific event in my family and my family's reaction to it as we sought God's face and comfort.

The next four chapters deal with incidents from the life of Elijah. Elijah was one of the greatest servants of the Lord and yet he experienced one of the severest bouts of depression recorded in Holy Scripture. How this came about and how God dealt with his servant and restored him is the subject of chapters 3, 4, and 5.

The remaining chapters reveal some other leading characters of the Bible who suffered grave hardships—John the Baptist (Doubt); Simon Peter (Cost); and our Lord Jesus Christ (Anguish).

It is not intended that the book be read as if it were a continuous, developing story as in (say) a novel or a biography. Each of the chapters is a separate study and readers will therefore find some repetition from chapter to chapter.

The chapters might be useful as weekly assignments for a study group such as a Sunday School class, and I have added some suggested discussion questions at the end for those who wish to use them in this way. Bible references are from the New International Version unless otherwise stated. Any emphases are mine.

Throughout my preaching ministry I have been indebted to innumerable gifted preachers, Bible commentators, and authors and I have learned much from them as well as from my own experience. In those places in the text where I have included direct quotations I have endeavored to acknowledge the source. If I have inadvertently neglected to do so then I will correct that omission in any future edition.

I have been honored to pastor four churches; two in the United Kingdom, and two in the United States. I cannot express enough my gratitude to the members of those churches for their love and encouragement which in many cases continues to the present day.

Finally, I wish to thank all those who have supported and encouraged me in this project including my two sons and two daughters, their spouses, and many of our friends, with particular mention of my younger son, Richard, for his enthusiasm, patient proofreading, and valuable suggestions. This introduction would not be complete without a special tribute to my wife, June, not only for the many hours she has spent at the computer putting this book together, but also for her unceasing and tireless support for my ministry throughout our forty-seven years of marriage. I therefore dedicate this, my first book, to June.

While this is a book dealing with some of the problems that may arise in the Christian walk, nonetheless—as I point out in the text—I would not exchange the Christian life for any other. To know the joy and peace of sins forgiven; the daily presence of Christ whatever the circumstances; to have a purpose for living surpassing all others (to seek to live for the glory of God); and to know that at the end of this life there will be an abundant entrance into heaven; such blessings give a deep joy which is beyond price.

My prayer is that these messages may be a comfort to readers who may be finding the Christian road "rough and steep."

Harry Kilbride
Davenport, Florida
June 2005

CHAPTER ONE

Tragedy

COPING WITH CRISIS—A PERSONAL TESTIMONY

Even though I walk through the valley of the shadow of death,
I will fear no evil, for you are with me; your rod and your staff,
they comfort me.

(Psalm 23:4)

At approximately 12:30 a.m. on Monday, August 15, 1994, in Bradford, England, an intruder broke into the house of my eighty-year-old widowed stepmother, Mary Kilbride, and battered her to death.

Mary had married my father when I was twelve years old, five years after my natural mother had died. My father and Mary subsequently had a baby girl, my sister Julia, who currently teaches at the University of Amman, Jordan.

Julia has always kept her own home near Bradford while living abroad, and in August 1994 she was back there to visit her mother and to celebrate her (Julia's) birthday on August 15th. Thus Mary was murdered on her daughter's birthday.

I heard the shocking news by telephone, first from my daughter Alison, then from Julia. Even with the seemingly uncontrollable

13

violence in our (so called) civilized countries today, I nonetheless found it hard to believe anyone would do such a terrible thing to such a harmless, frail old lady.

Over the phone my stunned and tearful sister described her last hours with her mother. They had spent a beautiful Sunday together. Crippled with arthritis and no longer able to get out to church Mary, and daughter Julia had read the Bible, talked of the things of the Lord, and finished up with a time of prayer. At 9:15 p.m., Julia left to go to her own home about a mile away, having assured herself that her mother had carefully locked the door for the night. Julia planned to be back the next day for birthday celebrations. It was not to be.

At 9:30 the following morning, Mr. Arthur Higgins, a seventy-one-year-old Elder at the local Brethren Church, arrived to visit his friend, Mary. Before it became physically impossible, Mary had faithfully attended the services at the Brethren Church, and before my father died in 1983 they had regularly attended together. Mary, who now had few visitors, looked forward to seeing Arthur who would visit when he could.

Arthur found the front door swinging open and its glass panel broken. Clearly something was wrong. Receiving no answer to his call, he went up to Mary's bedroom. Days later, and still trembling, he told me he would never get over the sight which confronted him. Suffice it to say that police later described it as a "frenzied attack, with a level of violence far in excess of that required to subdue an old lady." Arthur phoned the police, who immediately sealed the house and sent officers to tell my sister the devastating news.

My wife June was horrified to learn what had happened and, while not relishing the prospect of being left alone, she nevertheless urged me to be at the side of my sister for as many days or weeks as was necessary. So I made plans to fly to England as soon as possible.

When I arrived in Bradford I found that Julia was receiving loving comfort from her aunt (Mary's sister-in-law) and a cousin. They greeted me with the news that an arrest had been made. Richard Whelan, an eighteen-year-old youth who lived only two houses from Mary, had been picked up for questioning and was discovered to have her purse and keys in his pocket. An examination of his bedroom revealed lead from around the glass panel in Mary's front door and other incriminating evidence.

At first he claimed to have found the purse in the street, but when confronted with the fact that his fingerprints were on the door, in the hallway, the bedroom, and elsewhere, he changed his story. He then claimed that he had been returning home from an evening drinking in the local pub, and seeing Mary's door open and damaged went in to investigate and found her body. He said that in a panic he fled the scene, impulsively taking her purse and keys. He told no one about what he had found and went to work as usual the next day.

The police did not believe this story and charged him with Mary's murder. The police theory is that he broke the glass panel and crawled through with intent to steal. Perhaps Mary was disturbed by the noise and he murdered her to silence her, for she would have recognized him. The murderer stole twenty pounds (approximately thirty dollars).

THE QUESTIONS

When an event such as this occurs—especially to a Christian who daily trusted in God for protection—searching questions come to mind. Questions such as: Why did God not protect his child, so vulnerable and helpless to protect herself? Are not his people called "the apple of his eye?" (Psalm 17:8; Zechariah 2:8) That is, the pupil of the eye, one of the most protected parts of the body. Why then would God let this happen to one of his own? Is God not a loving Father?

Or did he not notice the incident because he was too busy with more important matters? Did it happen when God was, as it were, not looking? Was he caught off-guard?

Or did God want to protect her, but could not because he is not all-powerful after all? Did he watch the foul deed while wringing his hands in frustrated impotence?

Or was it that Mary had sinned in some awful way and this was God's punishment? In Jesus' time, as in Job's, that would certainly have been a favored conclusion (see Luke 13:1-5 and John 9:1-3). It is a theory that unfortunately is still around.

What about God's promises? What about those wonderful verses we draw from the Promise Box or read from our daily tear-off calendars? Allow me to give just two examples:

> I will lie down and sleep in peace, for you alone, O Lord, make me dwell in safety.
>
> (Psalm 4:8)

> He who dwells in the shelter of the Most High will rest in the shadow of the Almighty. I will say of the Lord, "He is my refuge and my fortress, my God, in whom I trust." His faithfulness will be your shield and rampart. You will not fear the terror of night, nor the arrow that flies by day. If you make the Most High your dwelling ... then no harm will befall you, no disaster will come near your tent.
>
> (Psalm 91:1, 2, 5, 9-10)

Is it any wonder that questions come to mind? To many it seems either God's love, God's power, or God's Word is called into question here. In other words, what people want to know is: where was God when Mary was murdered?

A RESPONSE

There are no slick answers to the deep questions raised by such an event as the murder of Mary Kilbride. In fact, we may never be able to give any complete answers—slick or otherwise—to the question why. Some things belong in the mystery of God's providence. Let me state as concisely as I can my beliefs about certain relevant issues, and how they mold my thinking on this difficult question.

16

The Sovereignty of God

I believe God to be both omnipotent and sovereign. That is to say, there is nothing he cannot do (consistent with his own holy character). Nor is there anything which happens in the whole universe that God does not control and direct. He could have prevented Mary's death and can prevent any other tragedy. He is not surprised by anything, he is not unaware of anything, and neither is he frustrated by anything whatsoever. Indeed, everything is overruled to further his own wise purposes. Yes, this includes every evil deed, including murder. Men and demons may violate his commands, but they cannot thwart his purposes. This is absolutely fundamental. (See Isaiah 46:8-11; Acts 2:23; 4:28; Ephesians 1:11.) I believe the Bible when it declares: "Hallelujah! For our Lord God Almighty reigns" (Revelation 19:6).

The Love of God

I believe in the love of God. Is the sovereignty of God a cold attribute unaffected by feelings of compassion? By no means! Scripture declares, "God is love" (1 John 4:8 and 16), and throughout the Bible we have statements and demonstrations not only of God's sovereignty, but also of his love. This love culminated in the coming into the world of the Lord Jesus Christ, who is God incarnate. Moved with compassion Jesus healed the sick, raised the dead, reached out to the untouchables, and was the friend of the frail and the fallen. Never once did Jesus use his power to afflict anyone; rather, his tears flowed at the grief of loved-ones and at the hardness of men's hearts. No one can read the life of our Lord Jesus and conclude that God is heartless. Quite the reverse! Not a sparrow falls to the ground—let alone a precious widow—but God attends the funeral and weeps. In love God entered into our sorrows, for was not Jesus the "Man of Sorrows?" He was despised and rejected, and taken by wicked hands and crucified. God's own Son was also murdered. If ever we doubt God's love, we must hurry to the cross, for it was for us Jesus died (Isaiah 53:3-6; Romans 5:6-8).

17

A Fallen World

I believe in the fall of man. Adam's sin brought ruin. God's perfect world became infected with greed, lust, pride, violence, and corruption of every kind. Natural disasters and the pervasive wickedness of man bear testimony that something has gone wrong. Disease and death, sin and suffering, are part of the human experience.

Are Christians exempt? No. I believe Christians are subject to the consequences of the fall along with unbelievers. Do not the gardens of Christians grow weeds? Do not believing mothers bring forth their children in pain? Are Christians not subject to the aging process, sickness, and death?

Of course! All believers die of something. If Mary had not died at the hands of a brutal murderer, she would have died of something else. Neither are we exempt from our proportion of robberies, auto-accidents, layoffs, bankruptcies, infertility, untimely deaths, and heartaches of every kind. Anyone who thinks we are must be totally oblivious to reality.

Though I have no statistics to prove it, I have a hunch that Christians suffer as many disasters as non-Christians.

Do you think there were no Christians among the quarter of a million people who perished in the Asian tsunami in December 2004? We know there were. We have heard of entire congregations that were swept away on that terrible day.

Do you think there were no Christians among the three thousand who died on September 11, 2001, in the towers of the World Trade Center, at the Pentagon, and in that Pennsylvania field? We know there were.

Christian families lose children. I would have had two brothers but both were stillborn due to obstetric incompetence and neglect. Julia and I had a sister, but baby Susan died of a brain tumor aged two.

I write these things not to depress you but to warn you. There is so much false talk from the health, wealth, and prosperity preachers that some Christians are not prepared for tragedy, or they have to live in a world of make-believe. When any one of these things is appointed for us, rather than asking, "Why me?" perhaps we should ask, "Why *not* me?"

The Enemy

Not only is the Christian called upon to share in what Shakespeare's Hamlet (upon discovering his father's murder) called "the heartache and the thousand natural shocks that flesh is heir to," but the Christian may face additional trials because of his, or her, faith. These are the attacks of the enemy. Peter warns his persecuted readers who, "for a little while ... have had to suffer grief in all kinds of trials. Do not be surprised at the painful trial you are suffering as though something strange were happening to you. But rejoice that you participate in the sufferings of Christ" (1 Peter 1:6 and 4:12-13).

In various places in America one can visit a "Hall of Fame" for something or other—sports, movies, music, and so on. Well in Hebrews 11, we have the Hall of Fame of Faith. The heroes in the first three-quarters of the chapter experienced miraculous deliverance of one sort or another, but suddenly the picture changes:

> Others were tortured and refused to be released, so that they might gain a better resurrection. Some faced jeers and flogging, while still others were chained and put in prison. They were stoned; they were sawed in two; they were put to death by the sword. They went about in sheepskins and goatskins, destitute, persecuted and mis-treated—the world was not worthy of them. They wandered in deserts and mountains, and in caves and holes in the ground. These were all commended for their faith, yet none of them received what had been promised. God had planned something better for us so that only together with us would they be made perfect.
>
> (Hebrews 11:35b-40)

The Mystery of Providence

Now why one was delivered from the lions and another was not, I do not know. Why God allowed James to be beheaded but

19

delivered Peter, I do not know (Acts 12:1-19). Why my step-mother was murdered and my natural mother died slowly of heart valve disease, I do not know. Those are choices for God alone. I repeat, there is mystery in God's providence.

The Scripture says "How unsearchable his judgments and his paths beyond tracing out! Who has known the mind of the Lord?" (Romans 11:33, 34)

Will we only believe in God and trust him when we can understand all his ways? Will we only love him because he protects us from all harm and unpleasantness? That is what Satan said to God concerning prosperous Job. Read Job 1:8-12. Poor Job never knew the reason for his terrible afflictions, and when he asked God why Job received not an explanation but an explosion (chapters 38-41)! Will we love God for *who he is*, or only for the goodies he gives us? Are we Christians because we think it is an easy life option? Well I'm sorry, but it isn't. Jesus warned us that those who follow him must "bear a cross" (Luke 9:23-24; 14:27).

We may have problems understanding why God, who is both Absolute Sovereignty and Perfect Love, permits and uses evil things or allows his children to suffer, but he calls us to trust him in the dark as well as in the light. God does not have to explain his actions if he chooses not to. He is not obligated to justify himself. He has his reasons, and they are good and holy.

When Jesus' disciples saw a man blind from birth they asked him "Rabbi, who sinned, this man or his parents that he was born blind?" Jesus, in his reply, immediately refuted the commonly held view that suffering was a punishment for the sufferer's sin. He declined to discuss the immediate cause of the blindness, and pointed not to cause but to purpose. "Neither this man nor his parents sinned," said Jesus, "but this happened so that the work of God might be displayed in his life" (John 9:1-5).

When tragedy happens, the foremost question we need to ask is not, "Why has God allowed this?"—understandable as that question may be—but, "How shall I respond to it in a way which pleases God and is a testimony to the world?"

God's Megaphone

One reason why God allows the outworking of evil is to demonstrate to man how corrupt is the human heart and how weak is man to control it. Man is arrogant. He thinks he can ignore God and still run the world (and his own life) successfully. I firmly believe that but for God's common mercy upon mankind, there would be far more plane crashes, far more auto-accidents, far more innocent little children killed by drunk drivers or abducted, far more violent robberies, and far more murders of defenseless old ladies.

Behind the reality of this suffering world is the reality of the restraining control of a sovereign God. He permits some of these horrors and uses them as a way of reminding man of man's impotence and mortality. We sometimes refer to this as the over-ruling providence of God.

Just a week or two before my stepmother was murdered another elderly lady in the same neighborhood was sexually assaulted and stabbed to death in her home. As we watched the nightly news, it seemed as if there was a new outrage every day. Today's murder replaces yesterday's on the front pages—that is if they even make the front pages. Our governments often seem helpless. Our nations should be crying out to God for forgiveness and help. When God allows these things it is to humble man and to seek to turn his godless gaze to his Maker. They are (as C.S. Lewis put it), "God's megaphone," to reach deaf ears: willfully deaf ears.

This can be true personally as well as generally. People are understandably more ready to turn to God when tragedy strikes than when life is smooth and easy.

God's Purposes

Mary's murder had nothing whatever to do with her being a sinner. Of course Mary was, like the rest of us, a sinner, but a sinner saved by grace. Jesus, her Savior, had taken away her sin. She was, in fact, a very devout lady. Like her namesake in the Gospels, she sat daily at the feet of Jesus, learning and loving.

Going through her things later with my sister, we found her Bible, worn to the point of disintegration and with passage after passage underlined. We found pages of notes she had written from books read and sermons listened to. I was moved to find notes taken from my own sermons, which she had listened to on cassette tapes.

She seems to have had quite a list of charities and missionary works to which she regularly gave. Though her resources were meager, the Lord came first with his tithe. She had eagerly read the booklets I wrote, and sent me loving letters filled with grace, comfort and encouragement. She had asked me to send three copies of each booklet to her so that she could pass them to two friends without giving up her own copy. One of those friends was Arthur, the Elder who found her. The last booklet Mary had given him was on the subject of Jesus' cry from the cross, "Today, you will be with me in paradise."

When the Lord permits his children to suffer great sorrows, it may be for one or more of the following purposes:

- that faith may be shown to be genuine (1 Peter 1:7);
- as a testimony to the world seen in how the grieving one responds to the tragedy (2 Samuel 12:19-20; Job 1:20-22);
- to bring forth the fruit of enriched faith in that person's life—(Romans 5:3-4; James 1:2-4). Adversity is one of God's training tools to mold us to be like Christ (Romans 8:29);
- that the believer might be better able to comfort others who suffer (2 Corinthians 1:4);
- because God has some special purpose which he intends to bring forth from the event (see below).

All of these purposes were demonstrated in the events following the tragedy of Mary's death. Consider, for example, the first two.

The *faith* of my sister—shining through her tears and sorrow—was a *testimony* to neighbors, police, friends, and family. The police came to Julia's house almost every day to see us about one thing or another. They were as kind as they were efficient. One day, one of the officers expressed himself forcefully regarding the accused. There is no death penalty in England, but the officer clearly felt it would be appropriate in this case. My sister reacted with horror. "Oh, no; oh, no," she said with passion. "I feel desperately sorry for him. I can't imagine why he would do a thing like this. I know him. I've known him for years. My mother was always kind to him. I'm praying for him. I really am." The officers listened to this with incredulity.

The Memorial Service was held in the little Brethren church. It was a service full of praise to God and joy that Mary is with her Lord Jesus in heaven. It was evident to those present—neighbors, police, friends and family—that though we grieve, we do not grieve as others do who have no hope (1 Thessalonians 4:13).

After the service and interment the immediate family gathered in Mary's house. It was the first time we had been allowed to enter the house as it had been sealed while the investigators gathered forensic evidence. In fact, although it was three weeks to the day after the murder, we could still enter only under police supervision. I wondered if it might be a very difficult, if not even harrowing, experience. It turned out to be otherwise.

Ten of us assembled in the living room. The three police detectives sat discreetly in an adjoining room. Julia's cousin, David, played the piano and we sang hymns. We sang: *Praise my soul the King of Heaven; In Heavenly Love Abiding; Great is Thy Faithfulness* and *The Lord's My Shepherd.*

I was then requested to lead in prayer. I gave thanks for Mary's life; for the blessed day when she trusted Jesus as her Savior and for the holy work she had done for him. Even in the very room in which we stood, she had taught little children the things of God. I praised the Lord that she is now in paradise, no longer weak, and old, and sick, but rejoicing in the sight of the Lord Jesus. I rejoiced at the happy reunions she is enjoying with loved ones gone before.

I prayed for Julia, that she would not remember her birthday as the day her mother was murdered, but as the day her mother entered heaven. I prayed that God would banish all evil from the house and fill it again with the fragrance of his Presence. Above all, I prayed that, according to his promise, God would bring great good from this evil and eternal fruit from this tragedy. I prayed especially for the accused: that he might be saved, along with his family. I pleaded for the restoration of backsliders, the salvation of the lost, and the re-consecration of us all, that we too might live out our few short years in the dedicated service of our Savior.

You may think it sounds like it was rather a long prayer. Perhaps it was. I don't know because I was too caught up in it. I do know this; all these praises and petitions were endorsed by the group with much assent and with heartfelt "Amen's;" that several wept; and that when we were done praising and praying it seemed as if the glory of God had come down and filled the house. If there had been any demons in the house, they were certainly gone now.

When we went to report to the officers that we were ready to leave, they were very still and thoughtful, and one was weeping. It was a memorable moment for us all.

God's Promises

Someone may be asking, "But what of those promises of protection? Didn't they apply to Mary?"

Yes they did. I believe them all implicitly. No harm can come to a child of God unless God allows it. We must take all sensible precautions, but beyond that I believe with all my heart that we are protected by angels and offered the peace of God's continuous Presence. (See 2 Kings 6:15-17; Romans 8:31-39; Hebrews 13:5-6; 1 Peter 5:7.) So: where was God when Mary was murdered? He was right there. Only One was deserted in his hour of death, and that One so that we would never be.

"You will not fear the terror of the night." Who says she did? Mary loved Jesus, and "perfect love casts out fear" (1 John 4:18). We imagine we would be terrified if an intruder broke into our home with intent to harm us. At least I do! But we don't know. Here is a very important principle: God gives us grace to face whatever we have to face, *but only when the time comes*. Not in advance as we conjure up nightmare scenarios in our imaginations.

The promises of protection applied to Mary, but we must remember that if God permits such evil, it can only be because he has some high and holy purpose in so doing. Such promises are conditional upon his purposes. Yes, our physical welfare is of great concern to our heavenly Father, but it is not his highest purpose. He has greater designs, such as, for example, our spiritual development and the furtherance of his kingdom. His ultimate objective is the glory of his Son, the Lord Jesus Christ. Sometimes, therefore, the lesser purpose must be made subservient to the greater and, ultimately, to the greatest.

Or, let us put it another way: do you recall that, as an example of promises which assure God's children of his protection, I quoted from Psalm 91? But I stopped at verse 10. Verses 11 and 12 say,

> For he will command his angels concerning you to guard you in all your ways; they will lift you up in their hands, so that you will not strike your foot against a stone.

Do these words remind you of anything? Satan quoted these verses when he tempted Jesus in the wilderness. Obviously this Psalm, and the divine protection promised therein, applied to God's own Son more than to anyone. God's greatest love is for his Son. Yet notwithstanding that promise of protection, God delivered even Jesus up to evil men who crucified him. Why would God do that? Because it was his great and wonderful purpose to save an immeasurable number of lost sinners through the death of his Son. The cross was the most evil act of all time and yet the most glorious. For all eternity elect angels and blood-bought sinners will gaze upon the wounds of Christ and glorify Father, Son, and Spirit, in the amazing story of redemption (Revelation 5:11-14).

As I ponder the murder of Mary, one of God's special children, I think of that wonderful passage in John 12:23ff. On the eve of the cross our Lord declared: "The hour has come for the Son of Man to be glorified. I tell you the truth, unless a kernel of wheat falls to the ground and dies, it remains only a single seed. *But if it dies, it produces many seeds.*"

Do you not think that this principle applies not only to the Savior himself, but also to those who belong to him, follow in his footsteps, and share his sufferings. I believe so.

25

God's Mercies

There were mercies surrounding even Mary's murder itself.

It was merciful, was it not, that Julia was at home in England. At the time she was pursuing doctoral studies in Jordan where, as I have said previously, she now teaches. Had her mother been murdered while Julia was away, might she not have always tortured herself with the thought, "Oh, if only I had not signed up for that PhD course. If only I had been in Bradford to be near my mother, this would not have taken place." But she was in Bradford.

How merciful that she had that lovely day with her mother, much of it around the word of God, and the final minutes spent together in prayer. Those will be her last memories of her mother until they are reunited in heaven.

Heaven—ah, yes, it was to that glorious country Mary Kilbride was so suddenly transported on August 15, 1994. I say suddenly. We have every reason to believe it was so. There were no signs of a struggle. It seems a dreadful way to die, but no death is nice. Death is an enemy. On the cross Jesus conquered it. When he returns he will destroy it. Is a slow, lingering death more to be desired? It is hard to say so.

We know the horrible thing which did happen. We cannot know what protracted suffering may have been avoided; especially for someone who was eighty-years-old and almost bent double with arthritis. When facing the prospect of violent death, the Apostle Paul looked beyond it and expressed himself eager, "to depart and be with Christ, which is better by far" (Philippians 1:23).

In sixteenth century England many faithful men and women died violently and cruelly for their faith. One of them was Oxford scholar John Bradford. Described by contemporaries as "a bold, intrepid, sweet, earnest preacher," he was imprisoned in the Tower of London before being sentenced to be burnt at Smithfield. As he and a young pastor were being led to the place of execution, he noticed his colleague trembling. "Cheer up, brother," said the older saint, "we shall have a merry supper with the Lord tonight, you and I."

And I believe that before her murderer had finished washing his bloodstained hands in her bathroom washbasin, Mary was with Jesus. She had gone to bed expecting to enjoy a birthday lunch with her daughter the next day, but God had other plans. Instead she was to have a "merry supper" with her Savior and her husband (my dad), and with her brother and many others gathered to welcome her "home." And when poor Arthur entered and gazed upon that awful scene the next morning, she had for several hours been enjoying the peace and beauty of Paradise.

Arthur found her. What a mercy that it wasn't Julia. If Arthur will never get over it, what would it have been like for her daughter to find her mother. The odds on Julia finding her mother must have been very high. I cannot help thinking that God spared my sister that Monday morning, and entrusted the awful discovery to another.

There were mercies of comfort. Julia had her Aunt Ethel who had lost her husband, Mary's brother, the previous March. Ethel is a very practical, "get-things-seen-to" type, the salt of the earth. She provided meals, beds, transport, and comfort. Julia's cousin (another precious Christian) came up from Gloucester, and the two of them sat up together through dark nights when sleep failed and tears flowed.

Henrietta, Julia's very close friend, was in the middle of a globetrotting, backpacking solo adventure. She had been to India, Pakistan, and I don't know where else…and she had actually arrived in Amman, Jordan, to await the return of her friend. Seeking relief from the heat, she went to the British Council Library to read the newspapers. To her horror she read of the murder of Julia's mother. She flew home immediately, at considerable expense, and was with us from then on.

It was merciful that I was available and able to go at once to Julia's side and live with her through those four unforgettable weeks until she returned to her work. Had I been the pastor of a church at that time it would have been difficult, if not impossible!

Neighbors laid flowers on the doorstep; friends and colleagues called, some from far off parts of the world. Letters and cards arrived every day.

Fruitful Blessings

What noble and spiritual fruit might God bring from this ignoble and brutal act? Joseph told his callous and cruel brothers: "You meant evil against me but God meant it for good" (Genesis 50:20 NKJV). The Apostle Paul wrote, "And we know that in all things God works for the good of those who love him" (Romans 8:28). What "good" might God bring from this? We will watch with expectant faith.

Since we both reached adult life, Julia and I have always lived many miles away from one another—sometimes whole continents have separated us. Those weeks were by far the longest continuous time we have spent together since childhood. It was a rich and bonding time. Yes, we were brought together in sad circumstances, but perhaps we will need each other in the years ahead. Julia feels acutely the loss of her dearest friend in the loss of her mother. June assured her that she has both friends and family and a welcome in our home, in Florida, or wherever the Lord may lead us. My dad and stepmother would have loved to see us together—talking, weeping, laughing, praising, and praying.

Had Mary died in her sleep, I would have wanted to fly to Bradford for the funeral but, considering the tremendous expense, Julia might well have said, "Don't come, love. It is too expensive and my mum is with Jesus." At best a visit would have been for only a few days. Instead it was different. It took a murder for God to bring this about.

As I have written, unsaved friends, neighbors and police were at the Memorial Service—far more than usual, of course. Some traveled many miles. They heard the Gospel and were reminded forcefully that death is not far from any of us. It behooves us to be ready. In Mary's living room on the afternoon of the funeral I prayed that if any of us present had taken our eyes from the Savior, one of the blessings from this "kernel of wheat falling into the ground" would be a rededication of our lives to Jesus. There and then I rededicated my own life. Julia has since told me that she did so also.

When I said goodbye to the young detective that we knew the best, I asked him to take one of my booklets, "Today...with me in Paradise." He accepted it warmly and promised to read it immediately.

And what of the one accused, for whom we are all praying? When she was well enough, Mary used to have Bible Clubs for neighborhood children. They were connected to Child Evangelism Fellowship and were called "Good News Clubs." One of those who attended was the young man now accused of her murder. As he ponders quietly in his cell, maybe he will recall the message of God's love and give his heart to Jesus.

Perhaps other children, now grown up, or in their teens, have been given cause to remember Mary, her "Good News" and how she loved them so. Perhaps the Sovereign Lord will bring forth more fruit from seeds planted long ago.

CONCLUSION

May I finish this chapter by sharing a few exhortations with my readers?

1. I was deeply saddened at the sudden loss of my stepmother. You too may lose a loved one, young or old. Please make sure that the last memories you have of your relationship will be, like mine, sweet. You will carry them to your grave. If you have any rift, heal it *now*. I found that Mary had pinned up many photographs I had sent on the wall of her living room. I never knew that. I wish I had sent her more.

I always thought that Mary had many visitors, but Julia told me that was not so. Old people can be soon forgotten: out of sight, out of mind. It was a selfless sacrifice for Mary to urge Julia to go to Jordan and difficult for them both. I wish, therefore, that I had called Mary more often on the phone. I spoke to her about a month before she died. It is too late to call her now. I am grateful to God for what we did, but I can't help wishing we had done more. Do things for your loved ones while you can.

2. This brutal act was a deep shock to me. How grateful I have been for the theology I have learned and hold precious. It undergirded us. Friend: get a God-centered theology.

When tragedy strikes is not the time to begin your thinking and studying about the sovereignty of God and his providence. You need to be prepared. If you need help or suggested reading, please write to me. Doctrine is unfashionable these days, as is theology. "Doctrine" is just another word for "truth," and "theology" means "the study of God." When Christians no longer have an appetite to study God's truth or God himself there is something seriously wrong. How can you deal with suffering and sorrow unless you know who God is and what his priorities are? Jesus said, "... the truth will set you free" (John 8:32).

3. When adversity does strike us, how careful must be our response. The world is watching. Of course, we are not expected to like pain or welcome severe trials. We grieve. Nevertheless, if our faith seems to make no difference; if we are continually whining and saying, "Why me, why me?" it is a poor testimony, is it not? Also, young Christians look to us for an example. Julia's and my father, Reverend James Kilbride, taught us a sound theology, but he also modeled a life of strong faith even when the winds of adversity blew.

4. When our loving Father appoints for us afflictions, however severe, let us benefit from them as he intends. This is not automatic. Sorrow and suffering can make a Christian not better, but bitter. Let us draw closer to God, the great Comforter, "who comforts us in all our troubles, so that we can comfort those in any trouble with the comfort we ourselves have received from God" (2 Corinthians 1:4). So many today are suffering. What a compassionate ministry the Lord may intend for us, enriched from our own experience.

5. Above all, suppose you were to be suddenly taken from this world and called to meet Almighty God? Do you know *for sure* that you, like my stepmother Mary, will be in heaven? You can know.

Remember, Mary Kilbride is not in heaven because she lived a good life—though she did—but because she died, as she lived, trusting in Christ as her Lord and Savior. How wonderful if you, through reading this very personal account of her death, came to trust in him also.

POSTSCRIPT

On June 28, 1995 at Leeds Crown Court, Richard Whelan, aged 19, was found guilty of the murder of Mary Kilbride. He was sentenced to life imprisonment. There is no death penalty in England.

CHAPTER TWO

Hardship

WHEN THE BROOK DRIES UP

So [Elijah] did what the Lord had told him. He went to the Kerith Ravine, east of the Jordan, and stayed there. The ravens brought him bread and meat in the morning and bread and meat in the evening, and he drank from the brook. *Some time later the brook dried up* because there had been no rain in the land.

(1 Kings 17:5-7)

First we must set the scene as told to us in 1 Kings 16:29–17:7. Ahab, King of Israel, was a bad king—very bad. In fact he "did more evil in the eyes of the Lord..." and, "... did more to provoke the Lord, the God of Israel, to anger than did all the kings of Israel before him" (1 Kings 16:30 and 33).

Previous kings had introduced pagan practices and idolatry including ritual fornication and human sacrifice. Ahab not only encouraged these practices but also married a Baal devotee from Lebanon (the notorious Jezebel) and built a temple to Baal in his capital, Samaria. Far from rebelling against all this, the people of Israel—the covenant people of God—seem to have welcomed it.

Although the Lord is "slow to anger," chastisement was long overdue. On to the scene strode a hitherto unknown prophet of the Lord called Elijah. He announced to Ahab that there would be neither dew nor rain until further notice.

After Elijah had delivered this message, God sent him into hiding. He was led to a remote ravine on the east side of the River Jordan called Kerith. To drink, he was provided with water from the brook, and to eat, meat flown in by ravens. Every morning and evening they came with their "Special Delivery." So there was Elijah, a bit lonely perhaps, but safe from Ahab's soldiers and wonderfully taken care of. Just the place for a long, comfortable exile! However, it was not going to be quite like that. After a while, the brook dried up.

That must have been a very difficult experience for Elijah, because he had been sent to this particular brook. He had been told by the Lord that he would drink from the brook in "the Kerith ravine" (v3), and that he would eat the food that the ravens would bring. But now there is this severe problem; the brook is drying up. Whereas when he first arrived he could take a nice bath every evening and a shower every morning, he now watched the water level drop lower and lower until it was reduced to a trickle.

Now he must wait patiently with his bowl even to get enough to drink. No doubt he prayed earnestly about this deteriorating situation (for Elijah was a man of prayer), yet there was still no word from the Lord as to what he was to do next. Very trying!

What do you do when your brook dries up?

A COMMON EXPERIENCE

It seems to me that this is a picture of some of life's experiences. Something has flowed liberally for so long we assume it will always be there. Then it dries up. It might happen suddenly, or it might be gradual, but it is usually a very difficult experience. How do you handle it?

Might it be, for example, in the area of *finance*? When my wife and I say we have a cash flow problem, you know what that means! We are running short, we cannot pay our bills. Some of you, perhaps, have lost your jobs. Now what is going to happen? The brook has dried up. Or it may be in the area of business. You have run a very successful business, always expanding and investing, but it has suddenly reversed and now it is recession and retraction. You may even face bankruptcy.

Maybe you are at *college* and you used to do well, but now you are not doing so well. You had straight "A's" when you were at high school, but somehow or other at university it is much tougher, and the brook has dried up.

It might be in the realm of *health*. I heard a preacher say that as we grow older we get "lower and slower," and alas that is so true. Certainly, we lose an energy flow that we had when we were young. Is that how your brook is drying up?

It might be some *disaster* such as a hurricane, tornado, flood, earthquake or tsunami that has destroyed everything you possessed and your brook has dried up.

It may be in a *sense of purpose in life*. Some change takes place and you just begin to wonder if you are on the scrap heap. Maybe you have retired. You looked forward to it, but now that retirement has come your life doesn't seem to have much purpose. Some men have been "persuaded" to take early retirement and know this experience acutely. They are not yet ready for a Florida "Retirement Community." Anyway, there are hurricanes in Florida!

Some think that this only happens with retirement, but it can happen at other times as well.

My wife went through a difficult time as the children grew older and left the nest. You see, we have four children and it was a big chunk of June's life to raise them. In 1982, I left my pastorate in the south of England and became the Field Director of a European Mission. Of course, this meant we had to relocate. Only two of our four children moved with us, the time having come for the older two to make their own way in the world. Nicola, the youngest, was still at high school, but Richard had left school and was soon to go into the business world.

Thus, one memorable day, with an old bulging suitcase, off he went. Having waved a last goodbye I found my wife in the kitchen, crying. I asked a stupid question, "Why are you crying?"

She replied, "Because Richard has gone."

I said, "Well, isn't he supposed to go? This is the 14th, isn't it?"

She said, "No, I don't mean that. I mean he has gone for good now. He has left home."

I put my arms around her—trying to be tender and being anything but—and said, "Honey, don't cry. This is a day for rejoicing. Let's put out the flags. We have been raising children since forever, and now, gradually, they are leaving. Three down, one to go! Soon it will be just you and me. Won't that be wonderful?" (Mercifully she made no reply to that!!)

Those children had been her life. She bore them. She nursed them. She was the one they ran to when they cut their knees and needed comfort. She was the one who was there for them when they came in from school. She was the one who got up in the night over and over again (I sleep heavily!). She was always there. The children—her *life!* Her life when they were babies. Her life when they were at elementary school. Her life when they went through high school. But now they are leaving, she thinks, "What is my life now?" The brook has dried up. Many women have gone through the same thing.

It may be a *friendship* that has dried up. It used to flow bubbling and sparkling, so wonderful and refreshing, but it somehow went sour and now it has dried up.

Perhaps you are single. You may have had several relationships, maybe even contemplating marriage, but it did not happen. The brook dried up and you are lonely.

Or it might be your *marriage*. Where did the love go? What happened to the romance? The brook has dried up.

For some the problem is *spiritual*. Has your spiritual brook dried up?

Hymn writer William Cowper wrote:

Where is the blessedness I knew
When first I saw the Lord?
Where is the *soul-refreshing* view
Of Jesus and his Word?

Now each of the areas of life I have mentioned above is a special subject on its own, is it not? Each deserves special consideration—but I think they all have certain things in common and from this experience of Elijah we can derive some clues as to how we might handle the problem and also be of help to others. May I suggest five things.

First:

DO NOT DRAW WRONG CONCLUSIONS

Such as what?

"I must have stepped out of the will of God."

As if Elijah said, "Ah, this brook is drying up. I must have gone to the wrong brook. Maybe I misunderstood God's guidance. I thought he said Kerith but maybe it was not Kerith. If this was God's place and God's brook; the one he provided for me, and of which he said, 'You will drink from the brook,' I do not think it would dry up. I somehow stepped out of the will of God."

No, he had *not* stepped out of the will of God. He was right in the center of it. That was indeed the place where he was meant to be, even though the brook dried up. Just because you face hardship in your situation it does not automatically mean you are in the wrong place and not where God wanted you to be. It may be your conclusion which is wrong, not your guidance.

"I must have made God angry."

Another wrong conclusion would be to think we have angered God. As if Elijah said to himself, "Obviously God is punishing me. Not only is he punishing Israel for her idolatry but look, he

37

is punishing me too. The brook—*my* brook—has dried up. I must have somehow made God angry."

God was not punishing him at all. Just because your brook dries up does not mean that you have done something so wrong that God is having to chastise you. God does that much more rarely than some people seem to imagine. Always remember two important truths: first, *the Lord Jesus has taken the punishment for all our sins*—"there is now no condemnation" (Romans 8:1)—so any chastisement is not retribution but loving discipline from a caring father to a wayward, disobedient child.

The second truth is: *God is slow to anger* (Psalm 103:8). The rod of correction is his last resort, not his first. Israel had defied God for many, many years. If you have done wrong and made God angry, you will know it beyond a shadow of doubt. It will be a serious and continuous breach of what you know to be God's will and way.

When Jonah was told to go east and he went west, he knew what he had done … we always know. And then all God wants of us is that we forsake our sin and walk in his ways.

But you remember Job's friends, who came along and said to Job, "Come on Job, what have you done? These disasters would not have happened to you unless God was punishing you. What have you done? Own up. You must be a secret sinner." No, he was not. Satan delights to portray God as a harsh father who is quick to punish and slow to forgive. The *opposite* is the case. (See, for example, Psalm 103:8-14.)

We must not draw wrong conclusions.

"God is unfaithful."

A third wrong conclusion would be to question God's faithfulness.

As if Elijah reasoned, "God is unfaithful and doesn't keep his promises. He has probably forgotten about me. I guess I am just not that important."

Of course we might never actually *say* such things, but we might be tempted to *think* them. But listen: God had not said to Elijah *for how long* he would drink from the brook. God did not tell Elijah *all* his plans for him. God is never unfaithful. He never has been and he never will be. God could and would provide for his prophet and God can and will provide for you. He will never forget his promise. You are as important to him as Elijah was.

So if your brook dries up, the first thing you must do is to be very careful not to draw wrong conclusions. The enemy is a liar who, at times of hardship and trial, sows into our minds thoughts that are wrong.

SECOND:
REVIEW YOUR UNDERSTANDING OF THE BIBLE'S TEACHING ABOUT HARDSHIPS

Are you sure that you really know what the Bible teaches on this subject? Many of us come to wrong conclusions because we have wrong teaching. That is why doctrine matters. Some people are impatient with doctrine. Let us get on to the practicalities, they say. Yes, but we cannot understand the right practicalities unless we understand the right truth, and the right teaching. So we have to begin with that. That is the foundation.

Does God say in his Word, "My child your brook will never run dry? Now you have become a Christian you will never have a problem, never face a trial, and never have a disappointment?" Is that what the Bible teaches? Does God say, "Other businesses will fail, but yours never will. Other people will get sick, but you never will. Others will suffer tragic accidents, but never you. No family member of yours will ever be hurt. You will know neither hardship nor hospital; trials nor tears." Is that what the Bible teaches about hardships? I do not think so. But some preachers seem to preach this and some evangelists seem to promise it. I am not surprised that many Christian people are defeated, disappointed, and confused. This teaching is important enough that we must pull over for a moment to examine it further.

39

We will consult just one passage: Romans chapter 8, verses 18 through 29. As you read the following pages you may like to check it out in your own Bible. I would like to draw your attention to four important truths.

Believers must face trials

From verse 18, the Apostle Paul is looking forward to the future day when Jesus comes again to consummate his glorious kingdom. He writes, "I consider that our present sufferings are not worth comparing with the glory that will be revealed in us." Present sufferings? Yes.

Verse 20, "For the creation was subjected to frustration..." Frustration? Sure. Don't you ever feel frustrated?

Verse 22, "We know that the whole creation has been groaning as in the pains of childbirth right up to the present time ..." Groaning? Alas, yes.

"Ah, just a moment," says somebody, "but does that not refer to the *non*-Christian world and to unbelievers? Surely God will protect *us*, his children, from all that groaning, frustration and suffering. Surely it does not apply to us. Aren't you making a mistake?"

Well, look at the next verse, 23, "Not only so, but *we ourselves* who have the first fruits of the Spirit, groan inwardly..."

Verse 25, "If we hope for what we do *not yet* have, we wait for it patiently." Do you notice those two little three letter words? They are very important: "*not yet.*" Always remember, Christian people, we are living in the age of the "not yet."

So the first thing that we learn about trials and frustrations and "present sufferings" is: *trials must be faced by believers.* They will come even upon those who have the first fruits of the Spirit. Even upon Christian people. Even upon God's children.

The presence of the Holy Spirit

Let us move on in Romans 8, to verse 26, "In the same way, the Spirit helps us in our weakness." The second thing in this passage to which I want to draw your attention is: *we do not go through these trials alone.* We do have the Holy Spirit, and he walks with us through the shadows and the trials and is with us when the brooks dry up. He is right there.

> Even though I walk through the valley of the shadow of death, I will fear no evil, for you are with me; your rod and your staff, they comfort me
>
> (Psalm 23:4).

Purpose in trials

Thirdly, verse 28, "And we know that in all things God works for the good of those who love him, who have been called according to his purpose." Is this not one of the greatest verses in the Bible—Romans 8:28? Here is the third truth; *God directs and uses hardships and trials for "his purpose."* What is his purpose? To make us more like Jesus. Look at verse 29, "to be conformed to the likeness of his Son." That is what is meant by "good." He permits these hardships and trials to come upon us and directs them in order to accomplish this great and glorious purpose in our lives. By them God refines us and molds us to make us holy, and to make us useful; like our Lord Jesus Christ. It does not say all things are good. It says God works in everything for good.

One day there will be no more trials

We are living in the "not yet." We wait patiently for the "then" when Jesus wipes every tear from our eyes. This great passage is looking forward with excitement and expectation in phrase upon phrase. "We ... groan inwardly as we wait eagerly for our adoption as sons, the redemption of our bodies. For in this hope we were saved..." (Romans 8:23-24). Until then we take our place with suffering humanity. As I have stated in the last chapter, non-Christian businesses fail, and so do Christian businesses. Accidents and tragedies happen to unbelievers, and they happen to believers too.

From this brief excursion into Romans we have reminded ourselves of four very important truths about trials. Let me repeat them:

- Trials will come, even upon the believer;
- God, the Holy Spirit, is with us through such trials every step of the way;
- Our loving Father has appointed trials and directs them as tools to serve a good end—to make us more like the Lord Jesus;
- One day Jesus will return and such trials will be no more.

We can see all of this in Elijah's experience. "Some time later the brook dried up..." Now see what it says next, "... because there had been no rain in the land." In other words there was a drought and brooks were drying up everywhere. Elijah suffered the same as everybody else. God did not plan to interfere with that but he planned to use it for Elijah.

Why, if only Elijah could look beyond his own discomfort he would see God working in his life even in the drying up brook.

If, therefore, you are called upon to pass through a time of trial or deprivation, first be careful not to draw wrong conclusions and second, check out your understanding of the Bible's teaching on hardships.

THIRD:
NEVER FORGET THE RAVENS

You see, the brook dried up, *but the ravens kept coming.* And the ravens were tokens of the Lord's provision for his servant. God had said, "I have ordered the ravens to feed you there," and every time the ravens landed that proved to Elijah that God had not gone back on his promise and that God had not abandoned him.

Is there someone reading these words who is tempted to feel abandoned? Has your brook dried up? If so, may I ask you this: are the ravens still coming?

You have lost a friend? Well, do you have your health?

You have lost your health? Do you have a friend?

Your children have left home? Do they love you?

Have you lost a child? Do you still have a husband or a wife?

You have lost a husband or a wife? Do you have a child?

Have you lost your job? Do you have your eyesight? Can you see? Can you hear? Can you walk? Have not the ravens kept coming?

Have you lost your possessions, or your boyfriend or girlfriend? Do you have a bed to sleep on and food to eat?

Have you lost your money? Well do you have faith? The Apostle Peter says that faith is "more precious than gold which perishes." You may be a multi-millionaire, but you cannot take your money with you into eternity. It might buy you a palace, but it cannot buy you peace. Why, it cannot even buy you health, leave alone heaven. We all need to be reminded of that.

May I ask you, do you have faith in Jesus Christ as your Savior? Do you know that your name is written in the Lamb's Book of Life? Jesus said, "What good is it for a man to gain the whole world, yet forfeit his soul?" (Mark 8:36) When the call comes, as it will for every man, woman, boy, girl reading these words, do you know that your hope is built, not on money, possessions, or on any other thing but Jesus? Can you sing from your heart, "My hope is built on nothing less than Jesus' blood and righteousness?" What incomparable treasure it is to have faith and a place prepared for you in heaven.

Yes, the drought came, but Ahab's search parties did not. Though they hunted everywhere, they could not find Elijah. The brook dried up but the ravens kept coming.

Oh, my friend, give thanks for the ravens. It is tough when your brook dries up. God knows that. And you wonder, "What shall I do? How will the Lord provide? What is he going to say to me? Where will he direct me next?" He will tell you. But, are there no ravens? Are there no tokens also of his love and of his grace? Do not magnify the one, and forget and neglect the other.

May I give you a word of personal testimony concerning this? Some years ago the brook dried up for my wife and me. It seemed we had lost almost everything. There were moments when we were tempted to despair. Then we remembered this message and we started to look for the ravens. Oh, they were there: token after token of God's love and care. Furthermore, he began to pour down blessings upon us. Prayers answered which had been prayed for years. Gifts given that made us weep. Every day the ravens kept coming. Look for them my friend. They will be there. Lift up your eyes and see them. They carry love-gifts from God. *Never forget the ravens.*

FOURTH:

TRUST GOD, HE HAS A PLAN FOR YOU

God cared very much about his beloved prophet, of course, and had a plan for him. If you read the rest of the chapter—I Kings 17—you will read about it.

May I say, God cares very much about you too and has a plan for you. He chose you before ever you were born. He made you and gave you gifts and talents. Then he raised you in a particular way so that you would have a variety of molding experiences, some good, others bad. Nothing was by chance.

In due time, he saved you and gave you the gift of the Holy Spirit, all because he has a place for you in his work and in his kingdom, and a plan for you to live for his glory. As the old song says, "His eye is on the sparrow, and I know he watches you." Reminder: "And we know that in all things God works for the good of those who love him, who have been called according to his purpose" (Romans 8:28), and he will unfold his plan to you in due time. He is going to do that for Elijah, if Elijah will be patient and wait.

Listen to your Bible. Seek counsel from those who believe the Bible. Be in prayer, and his plan will be unfolded. He may move you on. He was going to move Elijah on. Elijah might have grown very comfortable at Kerith, but there was to be another stage and another place. Sometimes in God's plan, when we are at point "A", he does not always show us point "C" until we get to point "B." First "A", and then, "B".

We say, "Well, what is going to happen at "C" and "D" and "E"?

And the Lord replies, "I will show you when it is time."

So we must trust him and move on. His plans may surprise us. There may be unexpected twists and turns in the road. I am quite sure that God surprised Elijah. I do not think that in his wildest dreams Elijah would have predicted that he was going to be taken care of by a widow in Jezebel country. Yet that was what was going to happen (and what a story *that* is). You must be prepared to do anything, go anywhere, anytime, according to his will. Be open.

But, you know, God's timing will be just right. Think what might have happened if God had told Elijah in advance, just to satisfy Elijah's curiosity, what was in store for him when the brook dried up. Supposing God had said, "You see the brook going down? Well, I want you to stay here a while longer, until it dries up; and then you will go to Zarephath, in Sidon."

Perhaps Elijah would have gone too soon. Perhaps he would have left as soon as things started to get a bit difficult saying, "Well, I had better pack my bags and move on and see this new thing that God has told me about." But God did not want him to go too soon. There was a particular day on the divine calendar when Elijah had to arrive in Zarephath. It was going to be the last day, so far as she knew, of this woman's life. Elijah must not arrive even one day early.

If, on the other hand, God had not dried up the brook at all, perhaps Elijah never would have moved. *The only way God moves some of us is by drying up our brooks.* We get very comfortable and we think we know best and say, "I would like to stay here." Or, "I must have a job here," or "I would like to do this." And so sometimes, in order to move us on and into the next experience that he wants for us, at the right time he dries up the brook and tells us what's next.

Hidden Plans

Sometimes God hides his plans for us for a time, because he wants us to trust him in the dark as well as in the light. Never doubt in the dark the One you trusted in the light. We do not trust God because we understand everything he does in our lives. He owes us no explanations. We trust God because of *who he is.*

The Bible is a revelation of God. Who is he? He is El Shaddai, the Lord God Almighty. There is nothing he cannot do; no problem he cannot solve; no need he cannot meet. He is the Living God, the Lord, the God of Israel, the God of Elijah, and the God and Father of our Lord Jesus Christ. We know that God is good. We know he loves us with an everlasting love, has saved us, and will never leave us nor forsake us.

Jesus taught us: do not be anxious about tomorrow. Does not your heavenly Father take care of the little birds? And look around you at the lilies of the field, the little flowers, the wild flowers which only blossom and bloom for maybe a day and then they are gone. God cares about them. Do you not think he cares for you? Oh you of little faith, of course he does. Just trust him for each day (see Matthew 6:25-34).

The Apostle Peter wrote,

> Humble yourselves, therefore, under God's mighty hand, that he may lift you up in due time. Cast all your anxiety on him because he cares for you.
>
> (1 Peter 5:6)

Dear friend, has your brook dried up? Are you perplexed? Confused? Will you look at the ravens he sends you and say, "But I *know* he cares for me." Will you come back to your Bible and read again those unshakable promises and say, "God is faithful, I know it to be true." Then will you trust him? Not because you can understand all his ways (sometimes, as Scripture itself says, they "are past finding out"), but because he is who he is. Will you look again at your Savior, God's own beloved Son, bleeding and dying for you on that cross, and will you say, "Yes, Jesus loves me."

Anna Waring knew what it was like to suffer and to cry. She knew what it meant to be perplexed and to watch the brook dry up; but she wrote these words:

> In heavenly love abiding, no change my heart shall fear,
> And safe is such confiding, for nothing changes here.
> The storm may roar without me, my heart may low be laid,
> But God is round about me, and can I be dismayed?

Wherever He may guide me, no want shall turn me back,
My shepherd is beside me, and nothing can I lack.
His wisdom ever waketh, His sight is never dim,
He knows the way He taketh, and I will walk with Him.

Green pastures, are before me, which yet I have not seen.
Bright skies will soon be o'er me, where the dark clouds have
        been.
My hope I cannot measure, my path to life is free,
My Savior has my treasure, and He will walk with me.

Do not be anxious, Elijah, God does have a plan. He will show
it to you before long; be patient. Trust God, Elijah, not because
you know all the answers or have peeked behind the curtains of
heaven and know every last detail of God's sovereign purposes, but
because you know God. You know he is faithful.

I say the same to any blood-bought, twice-born child of God
reading these words. Maybe this chapter is one of God's "ravens,"
meant to be a token to you of his love. He will not fail you. Never.
Never! NEVER!

FIFTH:
LOOK UP AND LIVE FOR THE
GLORY OF GOD

We should not begin with ourselves and our troubles. Of course,
that is the natural thing for us to do. We are all inclined to do it, but
it is fatal. Our focus will then be in the wrong place. We could put
it this way: Elijah must not start with the problem of the brook or
even the provision of the ravens. He must look away from himself
and pray that God will be glorified in the repentance and restoration of Israel. God's great name is what matters first and foremost,
and not Elijah's bodily comforts.

Elijah must say, "Praise God. Look at this brook drying up. That
means God is keeping his word and withholding the rain and the
dew. Oh, may it please him to bring his people to repentance. May
Israel heed the lesson and forsake idolatry. May she return again
to the Covenant made of old and to her God. God will not forsake

47

me, I know. But if he should choose that I perish in the drought, so be it. I shall go to heaven and receive my reward, but let the name of the Lord be glorified."

Now someone may well be thinking, "That is totally unrealistic, Harry. No-one can be that way!"

Of course we cannot by our old nature, but when we were born again did we not receive a new nature? Does not the Scripture say, "If anyone is in Christ, he is a *new creation* ...?" (2 Corinthians 5:17). Were we not given the gift of the Holy Spirit, that through his presence and power we might glorify the Lord Jesus? What does the old catechism say, "The chief end of man is to glorify God." I wonder if we have forgotten that. Even better; did not our Lord Jesus teach us to pray first, "Hallowed be *your* Name; *your* kingdom come; *your* will be done, on earth as in heaven ... For *yours* is the kingdom and the power and the glory, for ever?" (Matthew 6:9-13 NKJV).

We live in days when, sadly, even the church has forgotten its message. Maybe that is why this last point seems so strange to many of us. We pander to the tendency to think that all that matters is *me*. What is in it for *me*? What will this church do for *me*? Will it meet *my* needs? What will God do for *me*? Me. Me. Me. Me.

Should not both you and I, above all else, seek the aid of the Holy Spirit that we might lift our eyes *away from ourselves* and have a window opened into heaven? There we will see, with the eye of faith, our dear Savior, the Lord Jesus Christ; King of Kings and Lord of Lords. There he is, at the right hand of God, ruling and reigning over all things. He is building his kingdom for all eternity.

Should we not be saying, "What is my life but a vapor? It counts for nothing without him. Soon it will be over and I will stand before him. All I want therefore is that he will make of me now whatever he will, do with me whatever he chooses, and bring glory to himself through me."

When our brooks run dry or we face any kind of trial; therein, and therein alone, will lay fullness of joy and peace.

CHAPTER THREE

Depression – Part 1

I'VE HAD ENOUGH, LORD

[Elijah] came to a broom tree, sat down under it and prayed that he might die. "*I have had enough, Lord*," he said. "Take my life; I am no better than my ancestors."

(1 Kings 19:4)

Have you ever been so low in spirits that you have wished to die? Have you ever been so despondent, so despairing, so weary, so frustrated that you have cried out to God, "I've had enough, I just can't go on. I'm at the end of my rope?" That is how the great prophet Elijah felt, as expressed in the Bible verse quoted above.

Depression is a very important and relevant subject, especially for those who are depressed! A few people are (apparently) never depressed. Most people are depressed occasionally; many people are depressed frequently; and some people are *so* depressed for so long that it has been diagnosed as a clinical condition.

Elijah was one of the greatest prophets who ever lived; a man of amazing courage and faith; a man of earnest and effective prayer; and yet, in the story we are about to consider, we will find him in (almost) suicidal depression. We will need three chapters to do justice to this classic passage and its subject.

This will not be a psychological treatise on depression. I am not a professional psychologist. This will be a study of Elijah's depression, and also, more importantly, a study of how God reached down to help him. How God lifted Elijah out of his despondence, met with him in a memorable encounter, and sent him on his way refreshed and renewed for further service.

Elijah, we are told in James 5:17, was *"a man just like us."* In I Kings 18 we see him on the mountain top—literally, emotionally, and spiritually. Now, in I Kings 19, we see him in the valley. Life is often mountains and valleys. By the way, if you are unfamiliar with the story of Elijah, I suggest you read 1 Kings 17-19 before continuing. In this chapter (a study of I Kings 19:1-4, 9-10), we will investigate the probable causes for Elijah's depression. The next two chapters will focus on the kindness and deliverance of God under the titles: *The Touch of the Angel* (v 5-8) and *A Fresh Encounter with God* (v 9-18).

May God help us to know ourselves, to learn what are the causes of this condition and the answers to it; and to be better able to understand and help others.

> Now Ahab told Jezebel everything Elijah had done and how he had killed all the prophets with the sword. So Jezebel sent a messenger to Elijah to say, "May the gods deal with me, be it ever so severely, if by this time tomorrow I do not make your life like that of one of them." Elijah was afraid and ran for his life. When he came to Beersheba in Judah, he left his servant there, while he himself went a day's journey into the desert. He came to a broom tree, sat down under it and prayed that he might die. "I have had enough, Lord," he said, "Take my life; I am no better than my ancestors." Then he lay down under the tree and fell asleep.
>
> (1 Kings 19:1-5)

DEPRESSION–A HUMAN CONDITION

I need hardly tell you that this depression of Elijah is not an isolated case in the Bible. The Bible does not whitewash its heroes.

Other great men of faith, other spiritual giants, had similar experiences. It appears to be a characteristic of our human condition.

We will consider some examples from among the "greats,"—first in Scripture, then in history.

Heroes of Scripture

• Job—is described in Job 1:1 as "blameless and upright; he feared God and shunned evil." We talk about "the patience of Job," and rightly admire his amazing faith as expressed in Job 1:20-22. We do not hear so often about his depression, and yet it is the book's dominant theme until near the end. In chapter 3, verse 1, we read, "After this Job opened his mouth and cursed the day of his birth." That is depressed!

Read the entire third chapter for a glimpse at this poor man's emotional pain. Consider chapter 6, verses 2-3, "If only my anguish could be weighed and all my misery be placed on the scales! It would surely outweigh the sand of the seas." Perhaps if you and I had suffered what he suffered, we would have felt the same.

• David—is described, in 1 Samuel 13:14, as "a man after God's own heart." David was the brave slayer of Goliath and the greatest king Israel ever had. The Messiah would be of the line of David and would sit on the throne of David for ever. King David was also the sweet psalmist of Israel. He was inspired to write Psalm 23, and so many other wonderful Psalms we read or sing. But if I wanted to turn to a second classic passage on depression other than this story of Elijah, I think I would choose Psalm 42 in which David expresses his feelings so vividly and his faith so movingly.

> My tears have been my food day and night, while men say to me all day long, "Where is your God?" These things I remember as I pour out my soul: how I used to go with the multitude, leading the procession to the house of God, with shouts of joy and thanksgiving among the festive throng. Why are you downcast, O my soul? Why so disturbed within me? Put your hope in God, for I will yet praise him, my Savior and my God. My soul is downcast within me … Deep calls to deep in the roar of your waterfalls; all your waves and breakers have swept over me … I

say to God, my Rock, "Why have you forgotten me? Why must
I go about mourning, oppressed by the enemy?"

(Psalm 42:1-9)

Have you ever known that experience, where it seems as if
one wave of trouble follows hard upon another and "sorrows like
sea billows roll?" That is what David experienced. But he talks to
himself (no, not a crazy thing to do), trying to lift himself out of
this pit of sorrow and expressing his unshakable faith in God.

• Jeremiah—was another great prophet; one of the greatest.
Jeremiah chapter 20, from verse 13, reads, "Sing to the Lord! Give
praise to the Lord! He rescues the life of the needy from the hand
of the wicked." That sounds like a good start.

But the next verse tells us what he was really feeling. "Cursed
be the day I was born!" Oh dear. Here we go again. What a sudden
change. He has been trying to pull himself up by his bootlaces. He
has been urging himself to "sing to the Lord" but he cannot do it.
He admits, "Who am I trying to kid? I don't feel like singing to
the Lord. It is a farce." So he gives vent to the real truth, "Cursed
be the day I was born!"

Then he continues, "May the day my mother bore me not be
blessed!" In other words, "Don't you dare send me a card saying,
'Happy Birthday!' It was a cursed day! I wish I had never been
born!"

The passage continues, "Cursed be the man who brought my
father the news, who made him very glad, saying, 'A child is born
to you—a son!'" I always feel very sorry for this poor messenger.
All he did was to bring Jeremiah's father the news. He is getting
cursed as well. "May that man be like the towns the Lord overthrew
without pity." (He is really on a roll now.) "May he hear wailing
in the morning, a battle cry at noon. For he did not kill me in
the womb, with my mother as my grave, and her womb enlarged
forever. Why did I ever come out of the womb to see trouble and
sorrow and to end my days in shame?" (Jeremiah 20:13-18) And
you think you get depressed!!

- The Apostle Paul—in 2 Corinthians 4, explains that things have not always been easy, and puts it like this in verse 8,

> We are hard pressed on every side, but not crushed; perplexed, but not in despair; persecuted, but not abandoned; struck down, but not destroyed. We always carry around in our body the death of Jesus so that the life of Jesus may also be revealed in our body. For we who are alive are always being given over to death for Jesus' sake, so that his life may be revealed in our mortal body. So then, death is at work in us, but life is at work in you.

So the great Apostle was not on "cloud nine," or up in "the third heaven," all the time. In fact, the letters of Paul reveal that he felt it keenly when he was hurt. My, how it wounded him when he was falsely accused, when he was let down, when he was deserted, when he was lonely, and when he was seemingly unfruitful.

Now none of these biblical heroes remained in this downcast condition. God delivered them all. David was right when he said "I will yet praise him, my Savior and my God." He did. Nevertheless, I am reminding you that at times even the greatest of God's servants passed through the dark valley of depression. If you and I experience depression, let us take heart that we are in the succession of prophets and apostles. We are not alone.

Heroes of History

Do you have heroes from history: men and women that you have read about and admired and even longed to emulate? I do. My top ones (as you might guess) are all preachers. I have discovered that most of them were also afflicted with bouts of depression.

For example: Martin Luther was given to depression. So were John Calvin and George Whitefield. One of my heroes is Charles Haddon Spurgeon. This great Baptist pastor preached to a congregation of five thousand twice every Sunday in 19th century London. His sermons sold twenty-five thousand copies each week and were translated into twenty languages. Yet this eloquent and successful servant of God knew terrible bouts of depression. Writing of it once he declared, "My spirits were sunken so low that I could weep by the hour like a child, and yet I knew not what I wept for. Causeless depression cannot be reasoned with ... As well fight with the mist as with this shapeless, indefinable, yet all-beclouding hopelessness."

Spurgeon said this affliction could be banished only by "a heavenly hand".

I have had the privilege of personally speaking with a few of the well-known Christian leaders of more modern times, and they have known dark times also. Maybe some of you would be surprised if you knew who, but others of you would be, like me, greatly comforted, because you would realize what good company you are in.

But let me mention one more:

The Lord Jesus Christ

We come now with reverence and eavesdrop as our Lord bares his heart in the Garden of Gethsemane.

> Then Jesus went with his disciples to a place called Gethsemane, and he said to them, "Sit here while I go over there and pray." He took Peter and the two sons of Zebedee along with him, and he began to be sorrowful and troubled.
> (Matthew 26:36-37)

It does not say he took Peter and the two sons of Zebedee along with him, and they all held hands and began to have a praise party. It does not say he began to smile and to laugh and to say to Peter and John, "Praise God! Hallelujah!" It tells us:

> ...He began to be sorrowful and troubled. Then he said to them, "My soul is overwhelmed with sorrow to the point of death. Stay here and keep watch with me."
> (Matthew 26: 37-38)

J.B. Phillips even translates it, "He began to be horror-stricken and desperately depressed" (Mark 14:33).

It seems to me then from both Scripture and experience that depression is for many, if not for all, a part of the human condition. It is not necessarily sinful. Our Lord Jesus shared our humanity in all its fullness—except sin. He never committed a sin, yet he was the "man of sorrows and acquainted with grief."

Of course, Satan loves to pile on the guilt, so if you or I are depressed, Satan will surely take advantage of that and say, "You awful, wicked sinner. Call yourself a Christian? You ought not to be like this."

Poor Spurgeon regarded his despondency as his 'worst feature.' He said, "… it is a vice. I am heartily ashamed of myself for falling into it, but I am sure there is no remedy for it like a holy faith in God." Perhaps that was why Jeremiah was trying to pick himself up. It is bad enough feeling depressed (when we have so much to be thankful for) without the Accuser, Satan, piling on the guilt as well.

So, before we zoom in closely on Elijah's story we will first consider in a more general way some of the possible causes for depression and then see if we recognize them in God's servant.

SOME GENERAL CAUSES OF DEPRESSION

Depression may be *temperamental*. Some are more prone to it than others. It is somehow part of their inherited genetic make-up. Some are born with a sunny disposition while others are more inclined to be melancholy. This is not a matter of praise or blame: it is a fact.

I saw a video program recently about hymn-writers, including William Cowper. Cowper was a highly-acclaimed eighteenth-century English poet whom God used to write such well known hymns as, *God Moves in a Mysterious Way His Wonders to Perform, There is a Fountain Filled with Blood*, and many more.

William Cowper had suffered in his younger years with terrible depression, and even had to be admitted to an asylum for some years. Having told us this, the commentator then asserted that after Cowper found Jesus Christ as his Savior he was cured of his depression. But he was not! He still sometimes fell into terrible depressions and had to spend time in the hospital again. Yes, even as a Christian.

Depression may be *chemical*. Many mothers know about post-partum depression, and that kind of thing. Our bodies are incredibly complex, and physical changes in the body can bring about very marked and mysterious mood swings. If you suspect this is true of you, I urge you to see your physician and have a check-up.

Depression may be *circumstantial*. The things happening can be so unpleasant that we cannot avoid becoming despondent. Unemployment, loneliness, prolonged illness, and painful grief would be examples. It seems to me our emotional consciousness can be like those places in the ocean where there are contrary currents. Deep down the flow is in one direction, while nearer the surface the flow is completely the opposite. Similarly we may be downcast near the surface because of unpleasant circumstances, yet deep down we never lose those things which make up our joy in the Lord (faith, gratitude, love, peace, and so on).

Depression may be *spiritual*. In this case we may even lose the joy of the Lord which once we knew. As I mentioned in the last chapter, the same William Cowper wrote:

> Where is the blessedness I knew
> When first I saw the Lord?
> Where is the soul refreshing view
> Of Jesus and His Word?
>
> What peaceful hours I once enjoyed,
> How sweet their memory still;
> But they have left an aching void
> The world can never fill.

There can be times when we feel so spiritually barren that prayer is very hard, worship no longer seems to warm our cold hearts, and we may even doubt our salvation. Of course, some would immediately conclude that a person going through such an experience must be in a backslidden state. Alas, we will always have to endure those who rush to such superficial judgments. Job had to suffer his friends doing the same thing.

I am convinced God sometimes allows the more precious of his saints to pass through such times of spiritual dryness and depression to draw them closer to himself—and to bring them to greater blessing.

Elijah will find that to be the case. Cowper's searching hymn begins: "O for a closer walk with God," as does David's—Psalm 42:1 and 2, "As the deer pants for streams of water, so my soul pants for you, O God. My soul thirsts for God, for the living God. When can I go and meet with God?"

Depression may be *diabolical.* We sometimes forget that a battle rages in the spiritual realm into which we have been brought by our new birth and faith in Christ. The enemy of souls assaults us and I suggest that depression is one of the weapons in his arsenal or, at least, things that make for depression. Do you ever sense a great oppression—heaviness—for which there seems to be no explanation? Could it not be an attack of the devil? I think so. Then the enemy follows that with (false) guilt, like a one-two punch or a two-pronged attack.

Depression *may* be *sinful,* as we shall see; or there can be sinful elements in it. Perhaps, with many of us, it all too often is. Unconfessed sin, willful disobedience, hurt pride, lack of trust in God, ingratitude, self-pity, bearing grudges, and many other sources of depression are of course sinful.

Finally, depression can be *holy.* What?! Yes, holy. It depends upon the source of it and the reason for it. I would go so far as to say that there can be times when it is actually sinful *not* to be sad and troubled and heavy of heart. Faced with sin and sorrow, cruelty and crime, disease and death, how can a Christian believer feel otherwise? Why else was Jesus the "Man of Sorrows," and why else did he urge that the way of true blessedness is found by those "who mourn?" (Matthew 5:4)

What did the Lord Jesus feel when he stood beside the grave of his friend Lazarus and shared the sorrow of the family? I will tell you: *Jesus wept* (John 11:35). What did he feel as he contemplated the rejection of the people of Jerusalem and foresaw the awful suffering which was to fall upon that city? I will tell you: *Jesus wept* (Luke 19:41-44).

Our world, our society, and even our churches are in such a mess that I think it is possible we Christians do not mourn enough! The problem is that when we do feel sad, it is usually for the wrong reasons, selfish ones. I know of nowhere in the Bible, by the way, that tells us that the chief end of man is to be *happy*. Rather, our goal should be to be *holy*; and if we are holy there will be things over which we grieve—especially our own unworthiness.

And is it not a holy thing to long for heaven and for the coming of our Lord Jesus, when he will wipe every tear from our eyes and establish a kingdom of peace, purity, righteousness and love, for ever and ever? The Apostle Paul says we *groan* as we wait (Romans 8:18-25). We should! You may not hear much about that nowadays. Such teaching is unfashionable. More on this subject later.

It seems to me there were elements of most of these in Elijah's depression. After all, he was "a man just like us." I think we will see that as we now look more closely at this sad but instructive incident in Elijah's experience.

A CLOSER LOOK AT ELIJAH'S DEPRESSION

In this examination we may find not only help for ourselves but also more understanding of others. I want to give you twelve words that may have caused Elijah to be suicidally depressed.

Reaction

Mount Carmel had been a high point in Elijah's life and ministry, a high point of emotional and spiritual excitement. It is all there in 1 Kings, chapter 18—a mountaintop experience. There, not only Elijah but also the king and all Israel witnessed a mighty demonstration of God's power. Fire from heaven fell upon his sacrifice. Elijah's prayers were wonderfully answered, the prophets of Baal were proved impotent and Elijah's ministry vindicated. After the consuming fire came the refreshing rain. Elijah instructed his servant:

"Go and tell Ahab, 'Hitch up your chariot and go down before the rain stops you.'" Meanwhile, the sky grew black with clouds, the wind rose, a heavy rain came on and Ahab rode off to Jezreel.

(1 Kings 18:44-45)

Jezreel was the location of the royal summer palace. It was eighteen miles away.

The power of the Lord came upon Elijah and, tucking his cloak into his belt, he ran ahead of Ahab all the way to Jezreel.

(1 Kings 18:46)

That was some run. Eighteen miles! Though we do not know how old Elijah was when all this happened, it seems certain he was not a young man. Yet he was so excited, he ran eighteen miles faster than a chariot. He probably should have gone into the Guinness Book of Records!

But then what happened? Nothing! It was all over. Everyone went home. No change. From climax to anticlimax: from high to low. Often life is like that following excitement. Don't you get the blues sometimes after a wonderful vacation when it's back to work? Or, what about weddings? All the excitement and build up, a wonderful day, then the honeymoon. But then what? Back to work, back to cooking and cleaning and adjusting and trying to pay the bills. A weary grandmother said to a young bride, "Well, dear, it starts when you sink in his arms, but it ends with your arms in the sink!"

I think there is an element of reaction in a church sometimes after a wonderful evangelistic mission or crusade has finished (or a Christmas or Easter pageant). There were all the weeks, or even months, of planning and preparing; special classes, prayer groups, exciting music with augmented choir and orchestra. A frenzy of intense activity as the crusade draws near. Then the evangelist comes, many people respond and it seems like heaven. And then it is all over, and sometimes there is reaction. There is a bit of a let-down as the church tries to resume its normal steady routines and programs. After the fever comes a chill. I don't mean we should not have special times—especially evangelistic outreach—but rather we should be prepared for the aftermath.

Disappointment

Suppose our wonderful and exciting 'special effort' did not effect real and lasting change. Suppose, after all the faithful follow-up work has been done, the number of true conversions proves to be only a small fraction of those we counted in the heady days of the event. Then the feeling of let-down and despondency is all the worse. So it was with Elijah. He had been sure that if only he could have a great "event" and demonstrate to Israel, once and for all, the impotence of Baal and the power of Jehovah, they would forsake their idols and return to their covenant God.

And so it seemed at first. "The LORD, He is God," all Israel had cried as the fire fell. But it didn't last. There was no revival. There was no change. His dreams did not come true. His hopes were dashed. Ahab is still concerned with his horses and expanding his property. He is not concerned with religion at all, except false religion to please his wife, Jezebel. She is still there, along with her temple to Baal that had been built in Samaria: business as usual—Baal-business.

You see, miracles, like the miracle on Carmel, are soon forgotten, unless there is a miracle in the heart. But what a disappointment for Elijah!

We too can be depressed through disappointment. Maybe there is someone reading this book right now and you have been prompted to read it because your dreams have not come true. Your expectations have been unfulfilled. Your hopes have been dashed. It may be with regard to your job; it promised a lot but has given little. Or your marriage; where did the romance go? It may be disappointment in a political program or politician.

Or it may be, more importantly, in becoming a Christian. Someone led you to believe you could have heaven now; and sometimes it seems more like hell. We live, you know, in a world of sorrow. In this world we may have to face trials and tribulations. We long for heaven but we are not there yet. Here there is sickness and failure; mysteries we cannot understand; sin and sorrow; depression and disappointment.

Disillusionment

Disillusionment is similar to disappointment and often follows from it. Elijah says, *"I have had enough, Lord."* Enough of what? Well for one thing, enough of Israel. They had let him down. Their professions of faith were false, and the covenant that Elijah so passionately believed in was in ruins.

He had had enough of his ministry. Israel wasn't worth bothering with anymore. Do you ever feel like that? Has someone let you down? Maybe a friend? Maybe a pastor, or church leader? Maybe you are disillusioned with the church. What a bunch of phony, ungrateful hypocrites! Is that how you feel? I have certainly known a few congregations who have become disillusioned with their pastors, but I have also known a few disillusioned pastors and preachers. Just like Elijah.

Fear

We read, *"Elijah was afraid and ran for his life."* Elijah's name had been a byword in courage. Yet here he is running for his life from Jezebel. Can you just imagine what happened when Ahab got home. It says in chapter 19, verse 1, "Ahab told Jezebel everything Elijah had done." When King Ahab told his Queen about the contest on Carmel, the impotence and humiliation of the prophets of Baal, Elijah's taunting of them and, especially, the summary execution of all four hundred and fifty of them, I guess Jezebel just went ballistic.

> So Jezebel sent a messenger to Elijah to say, "May the gods deal with me, be it ever so severely, if by this time tomorrow I do not make your life like that of one of them."
>
> (1 Kings 19:2)

In other words: "Put 'Wanted' notices on every tree and in every market place. Issue his description to every soldier. I want him dead or alive." King Ahab seems to have had no control in the matter. Though Ahab wore the crown, Jezebel clearly wore the pants!

Elijah was afraid and ran for his life. Fear. My own experience, as well as my reading, has convinced me that fear and anxiety can be major causes of depression.

Fear of the *past*: skeletons in the cupboard that somebody one day will expose. We seem to live in a society today that is obsessed with trying to dig up dirt. (I wonder that anyone ever runs for office.)

Fear of the *present*. Some of us have no idea what terrible fears some people live with every day. What will today bring? Will it (their worst fear) happen today?

Fear of the *future*. What will become of me? Only God knows. Yes he does, and he also knows about the problem of anxiety. That is why over three hundred and fifty times God in his Word says, "*Fear not...*" and gives the reasons why. It isn't just a cliché.

Exhaustion

Elijah must have been exhausted, both physically and emotionally, don't you think? Eighteen miles to Jezreel: yes, but then ninety miles more. You see, when Elijah realized there was going to be no revival, but rather that Jezebel was determined to have his head, he took off fleeing for his life heading south. He traveled over ninety miles. Up and down rough and stony hills he went. On and on he went until he hit the desert, with every painful mile getting hotter and hotter. Beersheba was, and is, the last outpost, and he staggered on even from there. He must have been absolutely exhausted when he eventually collapsed under a little tree. He could go no further. "I have had enough, Lord. I have had enough of Israel. I have had enough of *this journey*. I can't go on anymore ... in fact I have had enough of *living!*"

Another major cause of depression is over-strain, over-tiredness and exhaustion. Don't we know it? And how many of you have ever said, "I have had enough, Lord."

"...enough of *this job*—I have had enough of this nonsense from this boss. I have been humiliated yet again."

"...enough of *these children*—I just can't take it any more."

"...enough of *these elderly parents*—trying to take care of them, trying to look after them. Nobody knows what it is like. I love them, but I can't do it anymore."

"...enough of *these responsibilities*—but I don't know how to get out from under them. I am between a rock and a hard place. Lord, take my life, because I can't go on."

How many exhausted preachers have said like Elijah, "Lord I have had enough of *this ministry*." Don't condemn them. You will not if you have ever been there. You see, we try to do too much because some of us cannot say "No." Sometimes too much is piled upon us by others. We become stressed-out and absolutely emotionally and physically exhausted. And then we are depressed. Is it any wonder?

Failure

Elijah felt he was a failure. Did he not say, "Take my life for I am no better than my ancestors?" What does he mean? Does he mean, no more successful than previous prophets? Ahab was the seventh king of Israel. It had been a sad story of apostasy, idolatry, and infidelity, all the way through. Other prophets had lived and preached and died, and seen no change. Things only grew worse. Now the Lord's prophets were being executed for their faith.

But Elijah had expected to be more successful. He really did believe that he was going to see a change, a "U-turn" in the spiritual climate of the nation. There was going to be an end to Baal worship and a re-dedication of the nation to God. But it did not happen and poor Elijah was plunged into depression. *He blamed himself.* He was a failure.

Why should he have expected to be better? Sometimes the depression is our own fault because of our own self-imposed expectations. We blame ourselves when we don't achieve those expectations.

During my formative Christian years, I had a wonderful pastor. I was preparing for the ministry, and he spent time with me and taught me theology; patiently answering my endless (and probably sometimes very tiresome) questions. I loved him. Sadly he became so depressed with a sense of unworthiness and failure that he would go and sit in the garbage can outside in the yard, and put the lid on his head. His wife would call me and she would say, "He has put himself in the dustbin again." And I would cry.

"No better than my ancestors." Why should Elijah have expected to be better? Was it pride we see here in Elijah? After all he was "a man like us," and sometimes we want to outshine others to feed our vanity. Some pastors (and their churches?) want to fill their pews or break baptism records or build that spectacular new facility, not for God's glory, but their own! Ambition can be good, but it can also be an idol. The craving for "success" can be legitimate, but it can be a slave-driving master. It is not then the Lord Jesus who controls us but the compulsion to out-score, out-shine, out-build, out-earn, out-drive, everyone we know. That is sin. Many on that treadmill are doomed to depression because there is always more and, anyway, the motive is wrong.

Sometimes, of course, it is others who expect us to be better. Better than our parents. Better than our brother or our sister. "Why can't you be like your brother?" they say, "Your brother got straight A's. Why can't you? Why can't you be like your sister?"

Can you believe, when I used to teach high school I had some parents who grumbled at their child if he, or she, came second out of about forty students. "Why weren't you first?" That was all they could say. Some people spend the whole of their lives trying to prove themselves or trying to please a hyper-critical father or match a high-achiever in the family. It is a recipe for a lifetime of depression.

If we belong to Christ, we should give him our best but leave the results with him. As Samuel Rutherford said, "Duties are ours, events are the Lord's." Never is that more true than with genuine heaven-sent revival. Revival was for God to grant or withhold. If it didn't come, why did Elijah blame himself?

Guilt

"No better than my ancestors." Does Elijah feel guilty for running away? Or for being afraid? Or for some other reason? Feelings of guilt certainly lead to depression. If we are guilty then let us come to the cross and let the blood of Jesus wash us clean. Let us forsake our sin and with God's help live a renewed life. We need be depressed by guilt not one moment longer than it takes to turn back to a gracious God. Satan, however, is very fond of loading us with false guilt, as we have mentioned.

Loneliness

"He left his servant there." Elijah only had one person with him, whom he left in Beersheba. Elijah went on alone into the trackless, waterless, desert. So often, when we are depressed, overwrought, or disappointed, we cut off contact with our friends. We say, "Oh, you don't want to be with me. I am not fit to be with. Leave me alone." But, in some senses, that is the worst thing to do. "It is not good," said God in Paradise, "for the man to be alone" (Genesis 2:18).

That is why the apostle Paul liked to have a team, and needed those who would stand by him. If you read the Second Letter to Timothy, you will read the poignant words about those who deserted him. "At my first defense, no one came to my support, but everyone deserted me ... but the Lord stood at my side and gave me strength" (2 Timothy 4:16-17). Do you remember how the Lord Jesus Christ admonished his sleepy disciples, "Could you not watch with me?"

Loneliness can be very depressing. We must not leave our friends behind and cut ourselves off. Sometimes, however, it is not our fault. Oh how depressed some of us have been because we long for a friend. God was planning to give Elijah a friend.

Grudge

We need to take a sneak preview into verses 9 and 10 for this:

And the word of the Lord came to him: "What are you doing here, Elijah?" He replied, "I have been very zealous for the Lord God Almighty. The Israelites have rejected your covenant, broken down your altars, and put your prophets to death with the sword. I am the only one left, and now they are trying to kill me too."

Don't you think he is saying, "I deserve better? That is what I am doing here. I deserve better than this, because of all the good things that I have done. I mean, look Lord, I have been very zealous for you. And the Israelites, they have rejected you, but I have stood firm. I have been faithful. I have preached the Gospel, and what thanks have I got for it? I deserve better than this. I haven't been treated right."

Do you know that this is the conclusion of some of those who have studied these things clinically? *Holding grudges is one of the main causes of depression.*

What sort of grudges?

"My job doesn't pay enough, I deserve better."

"I was passed over for promotion, and somebody else got the position which was rightfully mine."

"My family does not respect me, my spouse does not love me, my boss does not appreciate me. No one does. I deserve better."

"My children have grown up, they do not call and they do not care."

"I have been a faithful wife and a dedicated parent and this is the thanks I get—dumped like a piece of old garbage. I deserve better."

"I am young and confused but my parents don't understand me. They do not care. I have done my best but all they do is criticize me. Life is unfair. I deserve better."

"I have worn myself out for my church, but I am unappreciated. I think I'll quit. Let someone else do it."

Do you think that Elijah's complaint is really against God? Is he saying, "I know that Israel is unfaithful, and Jezebel is a cruel, murderous, idolater, but Lord you could have changed that. Oh Lord, you ask me what I am doing here; I have come with a complaint against *you*. You could have wiped Jezebel off the face of the earth. You could have brought a great revival and vindicated me before the people. But you haven't. You ask me, Lord, why I am here? Frankly, Lord, I'm here because I just don't understand it. Why does faithfulness go unrewarded while apostasy, idolatry, and sin, prosper? Ahab and Jezebel feast in their palace while I, your faithful servant, flee for my life alone in the desert. I think I deserve better."

Surely when we Christians complain at the way "life" has treated us, isn't that really complaining at the way *God* has? A grudge against life is a grudge against God, a sure formula for depression.

I am not saying that we should be indifferent to pain. Grief, disappointment, pains, of various kinds *hurt*. We feel them. We are not meant to be stoics. However, we believe in a wise, omnipotent, loving God, who loves us. We accept whatever he wills.

Self-pity

"I am the only one left." Poor me! Poor me! This was a terrible exaggeration, you know. What about those prophets of the Lord that Obadiah had saved, fifty in one cave and fifty in another? God is going to have to straighten Elijah out on that. He is *not* the only one left. But what if he was? Isn't that God's business? Wallowing in self-pity is very depressing, and when we do it we usually distort the facts.

Despair

It is as if Elijah has concluded that the situation is hopeless. He has done his best and it hasn't worked. Now he will surely be caught and die a violent death, maybe after being tortured first. Or he will be a fugitive for his few remaining years. Little wonder he wants God to take him home to heaven. What else is there to live for?

Despair is, perhaps, the ultimate depression. No hope. No way out. We shall return to this later, but let me say right now: *no Christian should ever despair. With God there is always hope. ALWAYS!*

Now in all this I am not condemning Elijah. God forbid. I have been there. I am not condemning him, or judging him. I am trying with you, in this first of three chapters dealing with depression, to analyze and diagnose the contributory causes, so that when depression comes to us or to another we might be able to, having diagnosed the disease, better look for the cure.

I myself am inclined to think that Elijah's depression had not one cause only but was a mixture of most of the factors we have listed thus far. Some were natural. Some were circumstantial. Perhaps some were sinful. However I believe one was righteous, which leads me to this:

Godliness

A sincere and holy desire to see the Lord's Name exalted and false religion banished. He had, therefore, a corresponding disappointment at the present state of things. For all I know, even his sense of failure may have sprung, at least in part, from an honorable expectation that the Living God would use this prophet, whom he had called into service, to a ministry of blessing. Any minister—any church—has a right to hope for that. Our God is the God of revivals.

CONCLUSION

Friends, let us then be slow to judge when we are confronted with someone who is depressed, or let us not judge ourselves too severely when we are depressed. And let us certainly never think there are always easy and glib answers. There is nothing more depressing when you are down than when somebody comes with some glib answer or cliché. Even verses of Scripture can be quoted in an insensitive manner.

Nevertheless, if we understand a little better how despondency can over*take* us, perhaps we can the better make sure it will never over*whelm* us.

As I have indicated, we shall explore much more fully in the next two chapters God's wonderful kindness in response to Elijah's condition. What does God do? Does he punish him? Does he fire him? Does he ignore him? Does he take his life—since that is what Elijah wanted? No. He does none of those things.

This is what God does to help him: first God sends an angel to meet his immediate physical needs. Then God calls him to a fresh encounter with himself. You see, Elijah had perhaps become too preoccupied with Elijah and everything was distorted.

My brothers and sisters, when you or I become preoccupied with ourselves we forget God and our perspective goes haywire.

And so Elijah had to come to Horeb, the mount of God, to have a fresh encounter with his God—and a renewed call. I sometimes wonder if that is maybe where he was headed. He was running *away*, yes, but he was running *to*. Don't run away. Run to. Run to God. You will never fly into outstretched arms as loving, as forgiving, as understanding, and as kind.

It may be that there is someone reading this chapter and you too "have had enough." You do not know how you can go on. It may be disappointment. It may be fear. It may be failure—or a sense of it. It may be weariness of life. Or maybe you have a grudge—a grudge from years ago still like a cancer in your soul. It may be guilt—paralyzing, torturing guilt. Whatever it is; run to God and meet with him again. Seek him with all your heart, because he is the only one who can help.

God loved Elijah. He had plans for him. He loves *you*, and has plans for *you*. I'll guarantee it.

He is waiting for you.

CHAPTER FOUR

Depression – Part 2

THE TOUCH OF AN ANGEL

[Elijah] came to a broom tree, sat down under it and prayed that he might die. "I have had enough, Lord," he said. "Take my life; I am no better than my ancestors." Then he lay down under the tree and fell asleep. *All at once an angel touched him* and said, "Get up and eat." He looked around, and there by his head was a cake of bread baked over hot coals and a jar of water. He ate and drank and then lay down again. The angel of the Lord came back a second time and touched him and said, "Get up and eat, for the journey is too much for you." So he got up and ate and drank. Strengthened by that food, he traveled forty days and forty nights until he reached Horeb, the mountain of God.

(1 Kings 19:4-8)

All at once an angel touched him" (1 Kings 19:5). This precious little sentence is one of my favorites in all of Scripture. It beautifully describes the tender kindness of God.

The "him" is the prophet Elijah. Elijah was, without question, a very great man. His name was a byword in courage, faith, and prayer. He was one of only two men allowed to go to heaven without passing through the experience of death. As the Lord Jesus Christ prepared to go to the cross, God chose two Old Testament heroes to meet with him on the mount of Transfiguration. Moses was chosen to represent the Law, and Elijah the Prophets.

But James tells us Elijah was "a man just like us" (James 5:17), and nowhere is that more clearly seen than in 1 Kings 19. Here we find him fleeing for his life from the murderous threats of Queen Jezebel until, in disillusionment, exhaustion, and with a deep sense of personal failure, he sinks down under the paltry shade of a little desert tree. Here, alone and despairing, he begs his Lord to end his misery and take his life.

In the first of these three chapters on depression, I considered what factors may have contributed to bring this great servant of God to such a low point of despondency and how we might diagnose the causes of our own depressions. We now go on to examine the response of the Lord to Elijah's condition and request. We will see how God met his immediate need through the ministry of an angel, before confronting him directly in an unforgettable Divine encounter amongst the rocks and pinnacles of Mount Horeb.

The encounter on Mount Horeb will be our study in the next chapter. In this chapter we will consider "The Touch of the Angel."

What kind of a touch was this touch of the angel? It was first of all:

A GRACIOUS TOUCH

This was not a touch of anger or punishment, but a touch of grace. Grace is mercy to the undeserving. Grace is being treated better than we deserve. Grace is to be forgiven when we deserve to be condemned. The Gospel is a gospel of grace. The truths of the gospel are sometimes referred to as the "Doctrines of Grace." Not one of us deserves to be saved. God does not owe us salvation as if it was a right, but he offers it to us through Jesus Christ. That is grace.

Now God had been remarkably good to Elijah. He had protected him for three and one half years from the wrath of Ahab and Jezebel while they hunted for him high and low. He had provided for him, first by ravens at the brook Kerith, then through a widow in

Zarephath. God had answered Elijah's prayers in dramatic ways. Prayers for the life of the widow's boy, prayers for fire to fall on the Mount Carmel sacrifice, and prayers for rain, had all been miraculously granted. Elijah's ministry had been vindicated in the sight of all Israel. Elijah had seen miracles.

Yet here we find God's servant behaving more out of fear than faith. He has left his post without permission and will eventually have to be sent back. His suicidally depressive claim—that he is no better than his ancestors and wants to die—sounds awfully like self-pity. When he eventually arrives at Horeb he does not come into God's courts with praise and thanksgiving but with self-righteousness and complaint. He has a complaint it seems, not only with Israel but with God himself.

We are not judging him as if we have not been just the same or even worse. At least this behavior was uncharacteristic of Elijah, which is probably more than can be said of some of us. Nevertheless, God might well have dispatched an angel to spank him—to snap him out of this despondency with a wallop from the proverbial "two-by-four." The touch could have been a touch of discipline—but it was not. It was a gracious touch, for as the Psalmist tells us,

> The Lord is compassionate and gracious, slow to anger, abounding in love ... he does not treat us as our sins deserve or repay us according to our iniquities ... as far as the east is from the west, so far has he removed our transgressions from us. As a father has compassion on his children, so the Lord has compassion on those who fear him; for he knows how we are formed, he remembers that we are dust.
>
> (Psalm 103:8-14)

Oh, how lovely it is when someone deals with you in grace. I recall as if it were yesterday an incident from my schooldays long ago. I was, I'm sorry to say, a very bad student. I did not do my homework and in fact was frequently absent from school without my father's knowledge. I was a rebellious boy. Consequently, I failed my final exams. I was sixteen and in order to graduate one was supposed to pass what was called in England at that time the "School Certificate." I failed miserably and was in disgrace. Of course, everyone was giving me a telling off, and justifiably so. My father was a pastor and pastors' children are, for some unaccountable reason, not only supposed never to fail at anything, but to get straight "As" and be, in every way, paragons of virtue.

On Sunday, therefore, everyone was telling me, "You ought to be ashamed of yourself." They were in huddles, glancing and glowering in my direction and "tut-tutting." I could hear them. "Oh! His poor father! Failed at every subject ... everyone else has passed except Harry Kilbride ... oh, tut, tut, tut, tut."

I was very depressed.

Then I saw my uncle heading my way. "Oh," I thought, "here comes another one."

He said to me, "I hear you have failed your School Certificate." I mumbled an admission.

I thought, "Go on then, have your money's worth. Put the boot in."

He asked me, "Is everyone telling you off?"

"Yes."

Then he put his arm around my shoulder and said, "Well, never you mind them, son. Just ignore them. They are not so perfect. There will come another day. You might surprise them yet!"

Then he gave me a big hug—and I began to cry. Sixteen year old rebels don't cry. Justice had not made me cry but grace did. Let me tell you something: I loved that man until the day he died and I always revere his memory.

How could he be so gracious? Because he knew that he had himself received grace, and because Jesus shone from his heart. Friend and reader; how do you touch the undeserving and the sinner? With grace, or with self-righteous judgment? A small kindness shown now may make such an impression that it will be remembered more than fifty years later.

First, the angel's touch was a gracious touch, but secondly it was:

A TENDER TOUCH

Poor Elijah was burnt out, preached out, stressed out, Jezebel-ed out, prayed out, and journeyed out. "I've had enough, Lord." He needed tender understanding and there is no one with such a supply and readiness to give it as our heavenly Father. "All at once an angel touched him," and it was a tender touch.

Not long after June and I were married in 1958, my young bride became seriously ill. Not only was there the shock of finding herself married to me, but it was also discovered that she had a problem needing emergency surgery. Our doctor, who was also our closest friend, counseled me concerning her recovery.

"Harry," he said, "you know with all the stress of being newly-wed, plus her very demanding teaching job, your youth work at the church, and this internal problem, June has become very run down. She is over-strained and exhausted. What she needs now more than anything else is a great deal of TLC—Tender Loving Care. Give her several doses every day."

Ah, yes, do we ever cease to need it? How frail we are. Elijah needed it. And his loving Lord gave it to him. I could fill pages quoting you verses which speak to us of God's kindness, gentleness, and love. But I will forbear. You can read them in the Psalms (for example), as we have seen. They are my constant comfort. I would prefer, however, just to turn your eyes upon Jesus, for he reveals the heart of God in a human life.

If you ever doubt that God is gentle, tender and caring, just think of Jesus. Jesus came to *reveal God to us* as well as to *reconcile us to God*. God is spirit. We find it difficult to take in the character of God from statements in the Bible—however plain. We need to see it fleshed out. That is the Incarnation. God became man. Jesus said, "If you have seen me you have seen the Father." Was there ever a man so kind? Again and again we read of him "moved with compassion;" to the widow, the prostitute, the leper, the outcast, the child.

At the 1987 National Prayer Breakfast in Washington, D.C., I heard Senator Sam Nunn of Georgia tell this story. Some years ago a young executive was hurrying through the forecourt of a busy city

75

railway station. It was rush hour and the station was crowded and he was late for an appointment. As he pushed and hurried through the crowd trying to make his train he accidentally knocked over the fruit stall of a blind boy. Apples, oranges, and the like, scattered all over the place.

The young executive hesitated but then hurried on. However, he had second thoughts and with a sigh he returned, resigned to missing both his train and his meeting. He began to help the boy collect up his dispersed merchandise and re-erect his stall. It took many minutes. At last it was done. As the boy thanked him he slipped a banknote into the boy's hand.

"You have lost business through my clumsiness," he told him. "Here is twenty dollars."

The astonished boy was speechless for a moment but then, as his benefactor moved away, he caught hold of his sleeve.

"Sir," said the boy, "Are you Jesus?"

Now some reader might say to me, "Harry, aren't you being sentimental?" To which I reply, "No. I am being *biblical*." I say again, read one of the Gospels. Any one. Was there ever a kinder shepherd?

When I was ordained to be a pastor (an under-shepherd) in 1969, I pledged myself to seek to be like Jesus. I have failed many times, and have a long, long way to go, but it still remains my deepest longing. He was so kind and full of compassion. Jesus was not weak. He was not a wimp. He was powerful and strong. Gentleness is not the opposite of strength but of brutality; and kindness is the opposite of cruelty, not power.

Let us be Gentle and Kind

God could have chastised Elijah. Or he could have ignored him or dismissed him ("No more service for you, Elijah!"), or granted his wish, requested from a distraught heart. But no, an angel touched him ... and it was a *tender touch*. I imagine that angel lovingly placing a pillow under his head, a cup to his mouth and, as the blistering heat of the desert day turned to the chilling cold of a desert night, carefully covering him with a cloak and keeping vigil.

Oh, my friends, let us all be kind and gentle as God is. The fruit of the Spirit is kindness and gentleness (Galatians 5:22). What a shame that Christians so often have the reputation of being harsh and judgmental.

Husbands and wives: let us be kind towards one another.

Parents: be kind and gentle with your children. I know fathers are not to spoil their children, and good discipline is an aspect of love. But please remember to be kind. After all, your heavenly Father is kind to you.

Pastors: be tender with your church members. How unkind some are to those in our own community who fall! I have known church leaders be so brutal towards a young unmarried girl who became pregnant that they seem more like ambassadors of Adolf Hitler than of Jesus of Nazareth. Galatians 6:1 says, "If someone is caught in a sin, you who are spiritual should restore him gently." Instead we often do the very opposite.

Churches: be kind to your pastor. He may sometimes feel like Elijah; and you don't even know it.

Is someone reading this and you are depressed and hurting? Like Elijah, you too have had enough. Are you broken? Are you burnt out? Have you cried out to God in your pain? Of course you have. He hears you. Yes, Jesus loves you. You will find he is far, far kinder than men. He will not turn away. The Bible says of Jesus, "A bruised reed he will not break, and a smoldering wick he will not snuff out" (Matthew 12:20). That means he restores that which is broken (he doesn't discard it), and he revives that which is burnt out (he doesn't trash it for another). He'll send an angel to touch you. It will be a tender touch. Thirdly, the touch of the angel was:

A PRACTICAL TOUCH

Angels are messengers. In the Bible they frequently come from God bearing a message, such as when angels appeared to Mary and to Joseph, or to the women at the tomb of our risen Lord. Here, however, it is more what the angel *did* than what he said that is significant. The grace and the tenderness took a very practical form. For one thing he saw to it that Elijah had a *good long sleep*, for Elijah was exhausted and needed rest.

If you are overtired, and especially if you are not enjoying enough sleep, you may have a tendency to depression. Some of us need more sleep than others, just as some get more tired than others. When faced with a fellow Christian who suffers from insomnia, some say, rather glibly, "Well, don't count sheep, dear, just think of the shepherd." Others say, "Start to pray and the devil will put you to sleep." So he might. The devil, however, might prefer to have you anxious during the night, drowsy during the day, and almost driven mad by the unfeeling comments of your fellow believers who have obviously never themselves suffered with this problem. I say, "Go see your doctor."

Some years ago when I was very, very overworked, very tired, and unable to sleep my doctor gave me a little medication to help me get off to sleep. Oh, how I thanked God for it. No, I did not have to keep increasing the dose. No, I did not become permanently dependent. God has granted us these "angels," and as long as they cause us no harm, they are a God-send. We need sleep. Elijah needed sleep. In this modern world of stress and noise it isn't always forthcoming.

He also needed some *food and drink*. I have no doubt he had neglected such things in his distress. Often, the greater our distress, the less our appetite. We consequently grow weaker. We read, "All at once an angel touched him and said, 'Get up and eat.' He looked around, and there by his head was a cake of bread baked over hot coals and a jar of water. He ate and drank and then lay down again."

Sometimes we can have mood changes because of other dietary problems. Maybe we eat too much, get over-weight, and then feel guilty, embarrassed, and frustrated. Others can be enslaved by the current fad of thinness. Some even diet to an unhealthy degree.

A Christian's body is a temple of the Holy Spirit and we should take care of it. It is not wrong to want to look our best. Nevertheless, we can become obsessed with the body to the point of idolatry, and especially with how we look to others. "Man looks at the outward appearance but the Lord looks at the heart" (1 Samuel 16:7).

Maybe you think this is all very unspiritual. Be patient, the spiritual will come. In the next chapter we shall concentrate upon the spiritual as we consider, "A Fresh Encounter with God." Sometimes, however, we need the practical first.

The Good Samaritan did not give the man who had been beaten up and left for dead a copy of "The Heavenly Thoughts of Matthias the Mystic." He bound up his wounds, poured in oil and wine, laid him on his donkey, took him to an inn, and paid for his keep until he recovered. And the first thing God did for Elijah—battered, bruised, and broken, and lying under this little broom tree—was to send an angel to give him a good dinner and a good sleep. The touch was not only gracious and tender, it was practical.

Could you be a practical "angel" to someone who is tired and may be depressed? It could make such a difference if you could do something for them. Could you do some yard-work for an older person, do their shopping (it might be even better to help them do their own), or decorate their home?

Little children are very, very exhausting. Could you take them for a couple of hours one afternoon and give that young mother a break? Could you baby-sit (for free!) for that couple one evening so they can go together to a worship service or to a concert or to a restaurant?

Many years ago, when June and I ran a thriving college and career youth ministry that we called "Young Disciples," a wonderful middle-aged couple called Sam and Jessie came to our home every Friday evening to look after our babies so that we could exercise this ministry together. What a blessing! They laid up treasure in heaven.

I am also reminded how, when we were raising our children, the "angels" were their grandparents. June's father and mother used to take them sometimes for a whole week or even longer. Those breaks from the children were wonderful times of refreshment for us. They winced a bit when number three arrived. Once it was four they said, "If you have any more we can't do it again." So we quit!

Sometimes it is through dark periods like this one of Elijah's that the practical "angels" come. One brings a bowl of fruit as a love token, another writes a treasured letter. One sends groceries or prepares a casserole while another gives professional advice free of charge. One invites you to their home while another offers the key to their country cottage or beach house. Where appropriate, monetary gifts arrive.

Reader: do you not remember such practical "angels" during some dark period of your life? Of course you do. You will never forget them. They were the hands of the Lord. "Are not all angels," says Hebrews 1:14, "ministering spirits sent to serve those who will inherit salvation?" So this angel came to serve Elijah and the service was very practical.

The "angel" may be a member of your family or a neighbor; someone in your church or a total stranger. Don't reject them, will you? Hebrews 13:2 exhorts us: "Do not forget to entertain strangers, for by so doing some people have entertained angels without knowing it."

The form of help may not be what you think you need nor the instrument who you would have preferred. Earlier in his life and ministry Elijah had been fed by ravens. Ravens were (ritualistically) unclean birds. Nevertheless, they brought good food and were the carriers of God's love. Then he was directed to a widow in Zarephath of Sidon. I am sure this was a surprise to him for Sidon was Jezebel country. Maybe he hoped she would be a rich widow who would keep him in luxury for the rest of his life. Actually she was a starving widow with just enough for herself, her son, and Elijah. But she was God's "angel," and God renewed the supply every day. Don't reject God's messenger or despise him, or her, will you?

Not only was this a practical touch but it was also, fourthly:

A PERSONAL TOUCH

There was actually somebody there. As he was sleeping he felt someone shaking his arm and saying, "Rise and eat." He thought he was alone, but there was this stranger who had obviously been hard at work as Elijah slept. Coals had been assembled and a fire ignited. A meal had then been cooked. Now God could have created this meal out of thin air at a word, but he wanted Elijah to have companionship and conversation.

We not only need rest and good food, but we also need friendship. We were not meant to go through this world alone. Depression is often caused by loneliness. Elijah did not have many friends but he had an assistant. However, he had left this servant and companion behind at Beersheba and had gone on alone into the desert. We do not know why. Perhaps he was so low he just wanted to hug his depression to himself. Perhaps he felt it inappropriate for the servant to see him this way and to hear this despairing prayer.

Nevertheless God said to Adam, even in Paradise, "It is not good for the man to be alone" (Genesis 2:18). Eve was created primarily to be his friend and partner. Marriage is God's primary answer to loneliness. Companionship should be the basis of marriage.

Now I know we cannot always choose whether to marry or not. Some have been married but have lost their loved one or been divorced. Then the loneliness may be worse and the pain harder to bear. God calls some to walk alone so far as marriage is concerned. He called his Son to walk that way. Our Lord Jesus had the same needs and feelings as you and me. He chose to remain single because (for one thing) his destiny was the cross. Nevertheless, even Jesus needed companionship. Yes: there were times when he went off alone—especially to pray. But usually he was with his disciples and other friends. When the crowds were deserting him in droves, he poignantly asked the Twelve, "Will you also go away?" In Gethsemane he admonished them, "Could you men not keep watch with me for one hour?" (Matthew 26:40)

The apostle Paul also denied himself marriage for the sake of the gospel. He was always on the road traveling, and he usually seemed to end up in jail. But he needed friends, and he traveled with a team. He hated to be left alone for long. Once, when he was in Athens, he desired to return to Thessalonica to see how the infant church which he had planted was doing. Again and again he was thwarted by some obstacle he interpreted as Satanic. Eventually he dispatched his team, being left, "at Athens alone" (1 Thessalonians 2:17-3:5 KJV).

He clearly did not care for it, but neither did he sit in his hotel bedroom wallowing in self-pity. He was out every day, sight-seeing, mingling with the people, and especially, sharing the gospel. My, what an antidote to depression it is to see someone saved through your witness. If the opposite of depression is euphoria, then I will testify that I have never been as euphoric as when I have been involved in any way in sinners coming to faith in Christ. It is the joy of the harvest. But if we do not sow, how shall we reap?

The same is true of friendships. Personal friendships need to be cultivated. We cannot wait until we are in a crisis or under the broom tree and then expect a friend to show up if we never bothered to foster any friends. It is good to have more than one friend, because sometimes erstwhile friends may desert us in our crisis—as they did the Apostle Paul.

Notice this about the angel, "The angel of the Lord came back a second time." That is precious. It was not just a flash in the (frying) pan. When you hit rock bottom, some will call or write once—and that is undoubtedly kind—but you never hear from them again. Others will come back a second time and a third and so on. Like this angel, they keep vigil.

Oh, what a blessing is a friend who remains loving and loyal no matter what. We need a friend who will still be our friend when we are behaving badly and may be a pain to be with. I know one such Friend "who sticks closer than a brother" (Proverbs18:24). Do you know him personally? His name is Jesus and he is the only Friend who can get you into heaven.

Fellowship in the Church

No one should be lonely who is a member of a church, and yet churches can be extremely lonely places. It is a tragedy. Some churches give visitors a hearty welcome at the door, have welcome cards for them to fill out, have this "greet-your-neighbor" session in the middle of the worship service, but it is all so mechanical and superficial. When the service is over no one speaks to you—even if you hang about until they lock the doors—but you see all the members gathering in their cliques and groups and you feel very left out. Do you know something? A crowded church porch following a service can be lonelier than the moon.

The essential marks of the early church included "fellowship" (Acts 2:42). It comes from a word meaning "to share a common life." The first Christians met together every day. They met in their homes. Fellowship is a missing element in many churches. Fellowship is intended for you by God and is a "means of grace." Lack of it can lead to spiritual malnourishment and to depression. Seek it, second only to sound and nourishing preaching.

By the way, may I take a little peek into Part 3 of our look at depression, which will be our next chapter? This angel is only a temporary friend. A stranger sent by God to meet Elijah's immediate and desperate needs: practical and personal. God has plans to give him a wonderful young friend and student who will serve him with devotion and be with him until the day he is taken home to heaven. His name will be almost the same—Elisha. Here under the tree in his loneliness, exhaustion, and despair Elijah, of course, didn't know about this future provision. God had not yet told him.

So, trust God, my lonely friend, he may have some lovely surprise for you later on. You cannot see his plans. Don't give up hope.

Be a Friend

You say, "Harry, I need a friend." Then go and be a friend to someone in need. Ask your pastor if he can suggest someone who might be lonely. I'll bet he will know. He should. There are people in prison who never, ever have a visitor or even receive a letter. There are people in Nursing Homes and Retirement Homes who are very lonely. There are people in their own homes who are very lonely. Elderly people are often lonely, yes, but sometimes so are young people, single people, and divorced people.

You say, "But Harry, I need an angel to touch *me*." Perhaps God is calling you to be an angel and touch someone else.

In my pastorates I would make it a practice to telephone individuals whom the Lord had laid on my heart, just to say, "I am thinking of you right now. I care for you, and I am praying for you."

You have no idea the reaction. Some would immediately assume that I must want something! (Money ... teach a class ... serve on a committee?) Others would cry because no one ever called them. I have called persons on Christmas Day and Thanksgiving and found them lonely and alone.

Don't be put off if you reach out to someone and at first they seem a little cold or embarrassed or even rebuff you. Many of us are shy or initially wary of an uninvited stranger. Perhaps their reflex reaction will be to imagine that their "constitutional right to privacy" is about to be invaded! Don't give up. God will use you. I will guarantee it. They may be in a state of shock that someone cares for them, but they won't forget. They will say, "An angel touched me today."

I once read a true story in my daughter's nursing journal. The writer—a nurse—worked in a very modern hospital with every technological aid. Beside each bed, built into the wall was a speaker and microphone. By pressing a button a patient could communicate with the nursing station several yards away and out of sight.

Little Johnny, aged about 8, was in hospital for the first time. After several hours he pressed his buzzer.

"Yes?" asked the nurse on duty over the inter-com. "What do you want?"

"Please, wall, I want my mummy," he replied.

Of course he did. What good is a *wall* when you are frightened and lonely and sick? The touch God gave to his sick, frightened, and lonely servant Elijah was a personal touch. It was also, fifthly:

A PURPOSEFUL TOUCH

The reason for the gracious and tender touch of the angel was not to comfort him, provide for him, and give him some personal care, only then to leave him under the broom tree. It was to enable him to fulfill God's immediate purpose for him, which was to journey to Horeb for a new encounter with God.

> The angel of the Lord came back a second time and touched him and said, "Get up and eat, for the journey is too much for you." So he got up and ate and drank. Strengthened by that food he traveled for forty days and forty nights until he reached Horeb, the mountain of God.
>
> (1 Kings 19:7-8)

Did you notice that little word, "journey?" "The journey is too much for you." May I imagine a conversation?

"Journey? Did you say journey? I'm not going on a journey."

"Oh yes, you are."

"But I have run away."

"Yes, but now you are going to Horeb to meet your Lord God, whom you serve."

"But I'm finished. I have no ministry left. I have nothing left to live for."

"You are not finished and you do have a ministry. The Lord will tell you."

"But I want to die."

"Maybe you do, but the Lord will decide that. He hasn't finished with you yet. You'll see. Now eat up your wheatibangs and your pancakes, and get up and go. Do you hear me? GO!"

That is the word to some of us when we are depressed. We need to get up and go. We can become paralyzed by pity—self-pity. Before we get our long term instructions from God, we may have to get out of this pit of dejection. Have some immediate goal or goals. Take a trip. Join the choir. Take a course. Write your memoirs. Visit a friend. Volunteer at the local hospital, library, prison, congressman's office, church office. Tell your pastor you want to volunteer: you'll do anything you can in accordance with your ability and strength. May I suggest to anyone in this condition: consecrate each day to the Lord and have assignments for that day. Don't stay in bed! Get up and GO!

Notice it was a long hard journey, this journey to Horeb. It took almost six weeks of very hard walking over rugged terrain. For toughness, the journey ahead was even worse than the journey before; much worse. The difference was that instead of running in a panic, Elijah would now be walking with a purpose. That is what God wants. We have no record that the angel walked with him. He certainly did not carry him.

Now if some of us had written this story we might have said, "And this beautiful angel lifted Elijah and carried him swiftly and easily, all the way to Horeb. It was as if a helicopter had picked him up and whisked him over the desert and the mountains to his rendezvous with destiny." Maybe Elijah would have liked that, but it wasn't God's plan.

God's ways are not our ways. He touched Elijah with grace and gentleness, practical provision and loving purpose, but then Elijah had to make this journey himself. Get up and go—and it wasn't an easy trip. The journey to Horeb is not unlike the journey to heaven—tough! Sometimes the stones beneath our feet are sharp and the mountains steep and the miles long. Like toddlers, we would like to be carried, but that isn't always good for us or them.

Nevertheless, I perceive Elijah striding out with a new determination. Refreshed and renewed, he now knows where he is going. He has received a touch from God and it was a purposeful touch.

That leads me to the final point. This was:

A DIVINE TOUCH

Did you notice that the writer changes from "an angel" (verse 5), to "...*the* angel of the Lord" (verse7): from the indefinite to the definite article. The expression "the angel of the Lord," in the Old Testament often refers to a temporary manifestation of the Lord himself. If this is the case here, then this "angel" (messenger) was none other than the Lord Jesus, the Son of God, making a pre-incarnation visit to someone in deep need (called by theologians, a "theophany"). Sometimes he did that. See Genesis 16:7-14, 21:17-19, 31:11-13, Exodus 3:2, Judges 6:1ff.

Whether "*an* angel," or "*the* angel," I cannot know for sure. What I do know is that God met Elijah's immediate need and sent him on his way. There was to be a place of rendezvous with the God he served and from whom he would receive fresh instructions (see next chapter).

What does this say to us? I can only tell you what it says to me. It reminds me that there are times when we become so depressed, so weak, and in such pain, that the Lord comes himself to us. Faithful and welcome though his emissaries are, this is an extreme situation which calls for something more – some*one* more. There is a gracious and tender touch needed here which even angels cannot supply. It is deep down inside. When we come to this, angels can help us but they cannot heal us. We are too far gone. We have been crushed almost beyond repair.

I say "almost" because there is no condition which does not respond to the restorative touch of the Divine Physician. There is no pit into which we can sink but he will not reach down and pull us out. He will not let us be destroyed. He loves us too much. He comes to us, just where we are. We cannot explain it, we can only experience it. There in all our pain and fear, our darkness and despair; deep, deep down, in the innermost recesses of the soul there is a touch—a touch so powerful and yet oh so tender. The touch is Divine. It is the Lord.

Never Forsaken

It is laid upon my heart to ask: among those reading this chapter is there a pastor or missionary or Christian worker? Do you feel like Elijah, "no better than your ancestors"—in other words, a failure? Maybe you haven't seen revival either. In fact the converts have been very few—and that one you felt sure was genuine has gone back. You are tired, disillusioned, and ready to quit the field. Are the enemies against you overwhelming you? Are the Ahabs and the Jezebels getting you down? Do you feel depressed, deserted, and alone? It might even seem that God himself has abandoned you.

NEVER! Did he not, just once, turn away from his only begotten Son so that he would never turn away from you or me? Every twice-born, blood-bought, child of God will never, never, NEVER be forsaken. He has promised it. He has proved it. Sometimes it might seem that way but it isn't. Look up, don't despair. He is hastening down to touch you. You are HIS.

Perhaps you have forgotten who and what you are: a child of Almighty God. Your adoption papers were signed in the blood of God's Son. If you are wounded and weary, why then, he loves you all the more.

Whatever the true identity of the angel, his mission was to enable and encourage Elijah to journey on. He must come to the holy mountain and confront afresh the One who called him into divine service, the Lord God Jehovah. So Elijah is headed for Horeb, a fresh encounter with God—and a renewed call.

Thank God he didn't miss the rendezvous with his Lord. Elijah might have said "No" to the journey, notwithstanding the ministry of the angel. How tragic that would have been. Thank God he woke up, ate up, packed up, buckled up, and journeyed on.

My prayer is that as this chapter is read it might be for someone the touch of an angel. A messenger sent from God to say, "I love you, and you are not finished yet ... come on ... let's go. We have eternal business to do together, you and me."

Fear not, He is with thee, O be not dismayed.
For He is thy God, and will still give thee aid;
He'll strengthen thee, help thee, and cause thee to stand,
Upheld by His righteous, omnipotent hand.

The soul that on Jesus has leaned for repose
He will not, He cannot, desert to its foes;
That soul, though all hell should endeavor to shake,
He never will leave, He will never forsake
—Richard Keene

CHAPTER FIVE

Depression – Part 3

A FRESH ENCOUNTER WITH GOD

…After the fire came a gentle whisper. When Elijah heard it, he
pulled the cloak over his face and went and stood at the mouth
of the cave. Then a voice said to him, "What are you doing here,
Elijah?"

(1 Kings 19:12-13)

Have you ever had such a wonderful and exciting experience
that you wished it would never end?

Elijah wanted the mountain-top experience of Mount Carmel
to go on for ever (see 1 Kings 18). It was all he had dreamed of,
preached for, and prayed over. The Lord God had demonstrated
his power, Baal had been proved impotent, and Baal's prophets had
been destroyed. The people cried as if with one voice, "The Lord,
he is God." Surely, Elijah supposed, national revival would now
sweep the country. It only remained to deal with that murderess
Jezebel, and a golden age would arrive.

It didn't work out that way. As we have seen in the previous
two chapters King Ahab went back to his obsession with posses-
sion, and Queen Jezebel not only survived but sought Elijah's

life. Israel's "conversion" evaporated like the morning dew. It was business as usual—Baal-business. Once more Elijah went into exile. This time, however, he fled the scene in fear. In the desert of the Negev, disappointed, disillusioned, exhausted, and alone, he prayed to die. To this suicidal servant, who regarded himself as an utter failure, life was no longer worth living. Faith had given way to fear, determination to despair, hope to self-pity.

But God was not yet ready to take him "home," for God was not finished with him yet. Elijah received the immediate and very practical help he obviously needed. An angel was dispatched from heaven to touch him. Oh, it was a touch so tender and kind. He was given sleep and food and encouraging words.

Elijah needed more than this, however. He needed a fresh encounter with God himself. He needed to go to Horeb and confront again the One who had called him years before and whom he had so faithfully served. He must pour out his soul (complaints and all) to his Lord.

My friend, maybe you are going through something similar to what Elijah experienced. The circumstances will be different, but the result is the same. Maybe you too have become exhausted, overwrought, and desperate to quit. You want out. Maybe you have been let-down, hurt, or even dealt with treacherously. Maybe you are lonely and crushed with grief or pain. The truth is: you too wish God would just take you home to heaven. Angels have touched you, and you thank God for each one, but you need something—*someone*—more. You need God.

Do you long for God? If only you could see him, hear him, know him. You long for that. Do you know something? You could not have a better longing! Some of us, it seems, only have that longing when we are down and desperate. "O God, help me," we cry. When all was well, we never did.

Have you ever thought what God's greatest ambition is for you? Is it to make you materially prosperous? Is it to make you successful? Is it to make you happy, so that you sing like a lark every day with never a care in the world? Well, it is none of these things. God's greatest desire *is for you to know him*, and knowing him, to make you like Christ.

Jesus prayed on the eve of the cross, "Now this is eternal life; that they may know you, the only true God, and Jesus Christ whom you have sent" (John 17:3).

It is one thing to know *about* God. It is quite another to know him—personally, intimately, deeply. That is his desire for each of us.

Now let's be honest, knowing God is not always the deepest desire we have for ourselves. Perhaps such a thing has never even entered our minds. We usually desire other things, and then we pursue what we desire. Only infrequently is it the pursuit of a deeper and richer knowledge of God. For some of us it takes a lifetime to bring our priorities for ourselves into line with God's.

Yet we learn with each fresh encounter that it is the sweetest thing we have ever known. Maybe gradually, maybe suddenly, the light dawns. *The knowledge of God is the pearl of great price.* Any other thing is flawed, counterfeit, and unsatisfying. This is what we really want. I have needed to learn it. I have learned more of it when I have been down than when I have been up. I learned it most when, like Elijah, I was helpless, fearful, and despairing. Then I learned it best of all. Strange, isn't it?

I am convinced that God allows us to go through such dark times as Elijah because he is going to use them to this great end. We would prefer to learn some other way (who wants to be depressed, who wants to suffer pain), but some of us don't learn "some other way," only this way.

I do not mean to suggest that painful experiences automatically draw us nearer to God. There is nothing automatic about it. They may do precisely the opposite. Suffering can lead to bitterness, and bitterness leads to godlessness. The choice is ours. Will what we are enduring drive us to God, or further away?

Elijah had a choice. He could have refused the journey and gone home to Gilead. He did not because he knew he needed God. He must find God. David declared, in the Psalm describing his depression:

As the deer pants for streams of water, so my soul pants for you,
O God. My soul thirsts for God, for the living God. When can I
go and meet with God?

(Psalm 42:1, 2)

The Apostle Paul, after all his journeys, converts, and churches,
had this one overwhelming ambition: "I want to know Christ"
(Philippians 3:10). Would that we all had the same longing!

Will you come, then, with me through 1 Kings 19: 8-18, and
let us see how we might have a fresh encounter with God, and
encountering him, know him as never before.

1. A SPECIAL PLACE

He traveled forty days and forty nights until he reached Horeb,
the mountain of God. There he went into a cave and spent the
night.

(1 Kings 19:8-9)

Mount Horeb and Mount Sinai are the same place. It was near
this mountain that God had revealed himself to Moses in the burning bush (Exodus 3:1-6). It was on Mount Sinai that God had given
Israel the Ten Commandments and other laws, making a solemn
covenant with them as his very own people. So Elijah, in his great
need, made the long arduous journey to Horeb (Sinai) "the mountain of God," to have a fresh encounter with God.

Does this mean we have to make a similar pilgrimage to a special
place if we want to meet God? No, and yes.

No: not necessarily. God is everywhere. Elijah knew God in
Gilead, his home state. There God had called him into his service.
He knew God in Samaria when he confronted King Ahab. He
knew God at the brook Kerith when God sent ravens to feed him,
and in Zarephath when God used a widow to take care of him,
and where God raised her son from the dead. Elijah knew God on
Mount Carmel when he prayed for fire, and then for rain. Elijah
even knew God in the desert when he prayed that he might die, for
God heard his cry and sent an angel. God is as near as breathing.

Paul, preaching to the idolatrous Athenians, said, "He is not far from each one of us. 'For in him we live and move and have our being'" (Acts 17:27-28).

Yes: in the sense that Elijah went to a specific place in order to seek a fresh encounter with God because he was desperate. He needed something extra-special. Consequently he went to an extra-special place. There is a message in that for me.

It speaks to me of:

The Place of Reconciliation

We must all come to the place where Jesus died. There is no meeting with God except through the cross. Jesus said, "No one comes to the Father but by me." That is why we pray, "through Jesus Christ our Lord." We cannot come into a deep knowledge of God until we are reconciled to him. Our sins have separated us from God. Yet God, in his great mercy, laid them on his Son, Jesus.

Have you ever put your trust in Jesus Christ? Have you knelt at the cross and believed with all your heart that Jesus died for you, and so believing given him your heart. You say, "Yes. I have come to the cross. I am a Christian, but I need a fresh encounter. I am down and almost out." Then, my brother or sister, you should still come to the cross. Come to the cross again and again. Gaze and gaze on the One who bore away your sins and loved you so much as to die for you.

> When Satan tempts me to despair, and tells me of the guilt within,
> Upward I look, and see Him there Who made an end of all my sin.
>
> (Charitie Lees Bancroft)

That is why the Lord's Supper—or Holy Communion—is so important. It brings us again and again to the meeting place of the cross. Could it be you will have your fresh encounter as you gather with the Lord's people and "break bread?"

Elijah's "special place" also speaks to me of:

The Place of Retreat

Elijah had left his place of service to journey alone to a remote mountain, there to meet with God. Many have found God in a new and deeper way by getting away from the place of disappointment and trial and visiting somewhere especially associated with fresh encounters with God.

For example: I had the privilege to preach a number of times at the great annual Keswick Convention in England's beautiful lake district. Beside a little gem of a lake, Lake Derwentwater, lies the market town of Keswick. It nestles at the foot of Mount Skiddaw and is surrounded by other splendid hills. Every year, for well over one hundred years, thousands have gathered for one week (now two), under the huge canvas tent, to be challenged to a fresh encounter with God. Many have made the pilgrimage to the Convention spiritually dry and feeling tired of life's journey. Many warriors have retired from the battlefield, wounded and weary, longing that in this quiet place they might find healing and restoration. Others have arrived, like Elijah at Horeb, with questions, complaints, disappointments, and disillusionments. Like Elijah, they "have had enough, Lord."

Yet they have come to Keswick because it is a special place. A place dedicated to the preaching of God's word. There God's people have experienced that challenging, comforting, healing, and life-changing word as it has reached deep down into their hurting hearts. Away from home, away from the battle, missionaries, pastors, husbands, wives, children, students, and all kinds of people have known a fresh encounter with God. It might happen in the tent at the close of the meeting: it might be alone afterwards up in those quiet hills and fells.

My downcast, spiritually dried-up friend, is there not some place like that to which you could go for a break—a summer camp, a convention, or a retreat-center? Consult your pastor. Most denominations have them and there are also others that are inter-denominational. The biographies reveal how many of God's servants had some sacred spot to which they retreated and where the Living God was revealed to them in a life-changing way.

We should also remember that when the Lord Jesus faced the demands of an exhausting ministry, he often "rose early" and went into the hills around Galilee's lake, and there alone in his own "special place" he kept his encounter fresh.

Elijah's journey to Horeb also speaks to me of:

The Place of Resolve

Perhaps, more than anything, this journey of Elijah to Horeb teaches me that life-changing encounters with God are not made casually. This is not for those who fit in a little time for it between supper and the start of the ball-game. Jeremiah 29:13 says, "You will seek me and find me when you seek me with all your heart."

Hebrews 11:6 tells us that God "rewards those who *earnestly* seek him."

Elijah was certainly doing that. From the broom tree to Horeb was a six week journey; a hard, mountainous, foot-slogging, desert journey. He faced blisteringly hot days and cold and dangerous nights. This lonely pilgrim might at any turn face flash floods, wild animals, or murderous bandits. But Elijah meant business. He was determined. He was resolved.

Your "special place" may be far away from home, or in your own bedroom. *Where* is not the point. What matters, I believe, is: *how earnestly do you seek him*? Is it "with all your heart?" Let me say it again: the deepest knowledge of God is not gained easily. It is not a "quick fix." A fresh encounter with God is not for the superficial, but for the desperate.

So, first we have—A Special Place. Now:

2. A SEARCHING QUESTION

And the word of the Lord came to him, 'What are you doing here, Elijah?'

(1 Kings 19:9)

I suspect this immediately took Elijah by surprise. After all, had *he* not come to Horeb to ask the questions?! Elijah was not only depressed he was mystified, as we shall see. Yet God opens the conversation with this searching question—and it is a searching question, isn't it? What are you doing here?

Sometimes we hear it when we are in a *bad* place. A place we ought not to be. What are you doing *here*?

Some Christians have heard that question when they were in a place of unwholesome entertainment. They were supposed to be having fun. Actually they were very uncomfortable because, you see, they were surrounded by that which was depraved or obscene. The Holy Spirit, quickening the conscience, asked, "What are you doing here, child of God? Is this a fit place for you to be?"

I cannot resist including here a true story from the life of one of my heroes, Charles Haddon Spurgeon, the great English Baptist preacher of the nineteenth century. Spurgeon spent the first six years of his life with his grandfather, the minister of the Independent Chapel in the Essex village of Stambourne. The young boy, learning that his grandfather was upset with one of his members who had taken to excessive drinking and bad company, went and boldly confronted the man.

According to the man's own testimony, the five year old Spurgeon strode into the tavern and, pointing his finger at the man (whose name was Thomas Roads), declared: "What doest thou here, Elijah? Sitting with the ungodly; and you a member of a church, and breaking your pastor's heart? I'm ashamed of you!"

Whereupon he walked away. "Old Roads" was convicted by the boy. He left his beer, went to a quiet place, and rededicated his life to his Lord. The change was permanent and he became a stalwart worker in the church.

Some of us have heard that question when we are not in a bad place, but in a *good* place—*but nevertheless, not where we ought to be.* Perhaps we have stayed at home when we ought to be in church. Perhaps, not wanting to miss that TV show, we failed to keep a commitment. Elijah had left his post. Was the Lord saying to him, "I do not recall withdrawing your commission to preach in Samaria. I am not aware that I changed your place of service or called you to retire. What are you doing here, Elijah?" That is a possible interpretation.

Some people hear the question because God called them to missionary service, but they have stayed home. Some husbands hear it when they are out yet again with "the boys," when they ought to be at home spending time with a lonely wife and neglected children. Some wives and mothers hear it when their precious babies are left day after day with strangers, not for economic necessity, but for greed or pleasure. "What are you doing here? You know this is not where you ought to be."

Elijah was certainly in a good place. There is no better place to be than seeking a fresh encounter with God. But if so, then why the searching question? I believe this was the first step in Elijah's re-education. Somehow he had lost his perspective. He had taken his eyes from God, and focused them on Jezebel and Ahab, and then upon himself.

He needed to be re-focused; and the first stage of this ophthalmic adjustment was when God spoke first, and did so with a question.

When Job—who surely could be excused for asking a few questions and who never did find out why he was called upon to suffer such terrible grief and pain—came before God, the Lord said, "Who is this that darkens my counsel with words without knowledge? Brace yourself like a man; I will question you and you shall answer me" (Job 38:2, 3).

After sixty-eight verses of questions from God to Job (at least Elijah only got one!), Job replied, "I am unworthy—how can I reply to you? I put my hand over my mouth. I spoke once, but I have no answer—twice, but I will say no more." (For this memorable encounter read Job, chapters 38 to 42.)

The answer to deep depression is a fresh encounter with God. And when we have that encounter, you can be sure it will contain a new comprehension of his greatness and our own utter unworthiness even to approach him at all. Perhaps Elijah arrived at Horeb expecting to ask God to explain himself. Instead God says to Elijah, "No. *You* explain *yourself*, Elijah!"

Does this mean he wants to push us further down? No. Actually a vision of the light of God's holiness and our own unworthiness does the very opposite—it lifts us up. It is *uplifting*. Does it mean he does not care about our depression? No: again the very opposite. He wants to cure it. Does it mean he doesn't want us to talk to him? No: yet again the very opposite. He loves to hear us talk to him. But there is a right way to come to him (more later). So let us go on to:

3. AN HONEST ANSWER

He replied, "I have been very zealous for the Lord God Almighty. The Israelites have rejected your covenant, broken down your altars, and put your prophets to death with the sword. I am the only one left, and now they are trying to kill me too."

(1 Kings 19:10)

Elijah does not imagine he is giving God information of which God is unaware. He is simply answering the question as to why he had fled from his appointed sphere of ministry, why he was so depressed that he wanted to die, and what was the anguish of his heart. True, there is perhaps a touch of self-righteousness (I have been very zealous...), the hint of complaint at Providence (now they are trying to kill me...), and a little self-pity (I am the only one left).

But we will not judge him. Many of us are far, far less zealous, and far, far more complaining. At least Elijah is honest. Before God, why be anything but honest? After all, he reads our hearts. We cannot hide our thoughts from him. Only before men do we feel we need to put on a mask.

"How are you today?" asks the usher at the entrance of the church.

"Oh, fine, just fine, thank you." We know very well he does not want to hear, "Well, actually, my heart is breaking." Or, "I have just been diagnosed with cancer."

When I first came to America, I did not know the system very well. Having driven hundreds of miles, I sank exhausted in the welcoming booth of the diner. "How are you this evening?" greeted the friendly waitress.

"As a matter of fact," I replied, "I have a migraine headache and I don't feel very well."

She was momentarily embarrassed and speechless. Then, her smile returning, she said, "Let me tell you about our specials tonight!"

So: we always say, "Fine, thank you, just fine." Even friends and loved ones rarely want to hear our woes. What can they do anyway? Consequently, we live behind a mask—or if we don't, we soon drive people away.

It is so very, very different with God. He wants honest answers. He wants to know. With him, we never need to pretend. He is the divine physician who invites us to pour out to him our pains and problems. Jesus is the burden-bearer, who invites us, "Come to me, all you who are weary and burdened, and I will give you rest" (Matthew 11:28).

That is why the psalms are so surprising—and comforting. We are almost shocked at the boldness and honesty of the psalmist. Again and again we glimpse the pain of the writer as he pours out his heart to God. Frequently he complains. Frequently he asks, "Why?" We read the psalms and say, "Here is King David, 'a man after God's own heart,' and yet he had the same problems as me. He too was hurt, betrayed, lonely, homesick, puzzled, tearful, ashamed, and spiritually and emotionally depressed. But God brought him through."

We will surely never be lower than the psalmist, and yet Psalms is the very book of the Bible which, perhaps more than any other, has lifted God's sorrowful servants out of their depressions by giving them a fresh encounter with the living God.

> I waited patiently for the Lord; he turned to me and heard my cry. He lifted me out of the slimy pit, out of the mud and mire; he set my feet on a rock and gave me a firm place to stand. He put a new song in my mouth, a hymn of praise to our God.
>
> (Psalm 40:1-3)

Let us go on to see how the Lord responds.

4. AN AWESOME DISPLAY

The Lord said, "Go out and stand on the mountain in the presence of the Lord, for the Lord is about to pass by." Then a great and powerful wind tore the mountains apart and shattered the rocks before the Lord, but the Lord was not in the wind. After the wind there was an earthquake, but the Lord was not in the earthquake. After the earthquake came a fire, but the Lord was not in the fire.

(1 Kings 19:11-12)

It is interesting that God does not answer Elijah's lament by patting him on the back and uttering soothing words of affirmation.

"I know, I know, Elijah. You have been wonderful, absolutely A+. I am really proud of you. You just have a self-image problem. Your self-esteem needs some adjustment."

Instead the Lord puts on a terrific show of extraordinary power. First came a hurricane. So powerful was it that the rocks of the mountain split asunder. It made our awesome Florida hurricanes seem like summer breezes. Perhaps it was the strongest hurricane in history, and as Elijah cowered in his cave he must have thought he would be buried alive. More was to follow. An earthquake. Apparently one of the most frightening experiences one can have is to be in an earthquake. Elijah had that. Then came lightning the like of which the prophet had never ever seen—or heard. Imagine what the thunder must have been like as it reverberated around the rocks and crevices of the mountain.

What does it mean, "The Lord was not in the wind?" It means there was no voice: no words. God was not saying something, he was *demonstrating* something. What? *His awesome power.* Remember, Elijah had everything out of perspective. He was acting as if Ahab and Jezebel were all-powerful and God was wringing his hands in impotent frustration.

At one time Elijah had focused on the Lord and feared no one. But his gaze had slipped. Like Peter walking on the water, Elijah took his eyes off his Lord and began to sink. He sank into one of the deepest depressions of fear and failure recorded in Scripture.

We too are only one glance away from falling. We must keep our eyes focused in the right place. "Let us fix our eyes on Jesus..." (Hebrews 12:2).

God needed to impress him with where the power truly lies. You say, do you mean God was showing off? In a way, yes. All of nature is God displaying his power and his glory. "The heavens declare the glory of God; the skies proclaim the work of his hands" (Psalm 19:1). It is interesting that when Abraham's faith faltered God commanded him to gaze into the night sky and count the stars—if he could.

When Job was confused and depressed and questioning God, his Lord reminded him of his mighty creative and sustaining power in nature. When the Lord Jesus wished to encourage his disciples to believe that their Father in heaven cares for them, he directed them to God's care of birds and flowers. The flowers have better clothes than kings and queens, and not one little sparrow dies but God attends the funeral.

Nature is God's canvas on which he paints examples of his power, beauty, creativity, provision, and loving care. We should not miss it just because we live in cities. Anyway, earthquakes, wind, and fire can be seen and heard in cities even where man's lights have hidden the stars and vandals have destroyed the flowers.

Have you ever been in the mountains during a storm? Have you been in the mountains at all? I love the mountains. Just from a geographical point of view, if I could live anywhere in the world, I would live in Grindelwald in the Bernese Oberland region of Switzerland. The town lies under the awesome north face of the Eiger (Ogre) mountain (13,000ft). Whenever I have hiked the trails of the Swiss Alps I have been reminded of the greatness of God.

Someone may ask; "When God's creation is so beautiful, why are there such destructive things as storms, hurricanes, earthquakes and the like?" Well, those things have come since the fall of man because all creation fell when man fell. They will not be present in the new heaven and the new earth. Now God uses them, as indeed he uses everything he permits and directs, to send a message. They are his wake-up call to a godless society. Untold thousands enjoy the creation but never worship the Creator or give thanks. Man is deaf to the quiet things, so God shouts.

Personally, thunder storms excite me. I always think, "My Father has come calling."

Sometimes even God's children need a shout. Instead of "magnifying the Lord"—that is, seeing him large in our vision—we allow him to be small to us. On our computers we view our documents as "windows." I can "maximize" a window so that it completely fills the screen, or I can "minimize" it so that it becomes a tiny icon in the bottom corner.

My troubled, downcast, despondent friend, who or what is God to you? Is he the Lord God Almighty who "fills your screen?" Or, have other things so dominated your vision that your sovereign God is just an icon: a verbal or visual image; a symbol? Perhaps for one hour each Sunday morning you "maximize" him as you sing *Our God is an Awesome God* or *How Great Thou Art*, but then he is once more reduced to the usual, insignificant, bottom corner of your life. Just a little picture!

I guess when Elijah emerged from that cave he had been woken up alright. It wasn't Jezebel who now filled his horizon, but Jehovah, Lord of heaven and earth. Why, the Lord who could tear the mountains apart could most certainly sweep Jezebel away with a word.

Is someone making *you* afraid? Who is it? Your boss at work? A close relative such as a father or a husband? My pastor colleague, is it that rich and powerful church leader who makes you tremble? My missionary friend, is it that local political tyrant? They think they have the power to lift you up or cast you down, don't they? They may even think they have the power to destroy you. Let me tell you something, *they have no power whatsoever except for that which your God and Father grants to them.* Their very next heartbeat is in his sovereign hand. The Lord Jesus needed to remind Pontius Pilate of this fact.

"Do you refuse to speak to me?" Pilate said, "Don't you realize I have power either to free you or to crucify you?"

Jesus answered, "You would have no power over me if it were not given to you from above" (John 19:10-11). Awesome!

The very first thing a fresh encounter with God will do for us is to magnify his greatness. Once again his awful majesty, sovereign power, and blinding holiness will fill our vision. When we are depressed—at least, when we are as depressed as Elijah was—it is frequently because adverse circumstances have overwhelmed us, enemies have all but destroyed us, and we feel helpless and hopeless. We will never get out of that pit unless we come to see again that, "with God nothing is impossible." He is able to deliver us.

He can still the storm, part the waters, crumble the walls, close the mouth of the lion, and liquidate the enemy. He is *the Lord.* Nothing is too hard for the Lord. The Apostles' Creed begins, "I believe in God the Father Almighty, Maker of heaven and earth." Do you really believe that? If you don't, no wonder you are depressed. There is no God. You have become—for all practical purposes—an atheist. But I am sure you do believe it. You just forgot. It is easily done.

After this dramatic and unforgettable theology lesson, God spoke. Let us therefore consider:

5. A GENTLE WHISPER

…And after the fire came a gentle whisper. When Elijah heard it, he pulled his cloak over his face and went out and stood at the mouth of the cave. Then a voice said to him, "What are you doing here, Elijah?" He replied, "I have been very zealous for the Lord God Almighty. The Israelites have rejected your covenant, broken down your altars, and put your prophets to death with the sword. I am the only one left, and now they are trying to kill me too."

(1 Kings 19:12-14)

Having been first overwhelmed by the awesome power of the God he served, Elijah now needed to experience what we might call the other side: the sweet and gentle tenderness of God. The whisper was so personal and intimate. How lovingly the Lord called to him. Nevertheless, the Lord asked Elijah the same question as before and—perhaps surprisingly—Elijah gave precisely the same answer. How can we understand this?

I believe the clue lies in the reference to "his cloak." Elijah was humbled by the experience of the earthquake, wind, and fire. He had no doubt cowered in his cave, scared out of his wits. Surely he would be either crushed to death or buried alive. Neither happened. Instead, in the solemn stillness which followed the crashing noise, he heard the Lord quietly calling his name. Elijah emerged from his hiding place—slowly, carefully, and with his cloak covering his face, lest he be destroyed by the Presence of the Lord.

Does this not remind us of Moses' encounter with God at the burning bush, when he was commanded to remove his shoes? Does it not remind us of the reaction of Isaiah to a vision of the glory of God (Isaiah 6:5), or of John to a vision of the risen and reigning Christ (Revelation 1:7)? We have already mentioned Job. We could mention others.

Friends: God does not want his children to approach him scared and trembling with fear. Hence the gentle whisper. But he does require us to approach him with reverence. Anyone who experiences a fresh and deep encounter with the living God does not approach him with flippancy, but with awe. It is a wonder of grace that we are not consumed, "… for our God is a consuming fire" (Hebrews 12:29). A confident approach is not contradictory to a reverent one. It seems to me that many churches, as well as many Christians, need a fresh encounter with the majestic holiness of God. We have become trivial.

It is, then, against the background of this true understanding of God in omnipotence and purity that we marvel at his grace. How can such a God know *me*, call *my* name, speak to *me* in a gentle whisper, and want for *me* nothing more than that I know him more deeply and more intimately than I have ever done before. It is amazing. Have you heard that gentle whisper calling your name? It is soft and full of love. Of course we cannot hear it if we never turn off the radio or television.

I used to see lapel buttons which declared, "Smile. God loves you." When you have the encounter of which this chapter speaks, you may more likely weep. You will weep with wonder at his grace. You will weep at the assurance that God loves you with an everlasting love, that your sins are gone forever, and that you can never, never be lost. The tears, of course, will be tears of joy. "Weep. God loves you."

But you may well also weep at the condition of the Church, as Elijah did at the condition of Israel. Gone now, I believe, were his self-pity, his complaint, and his self-righteousness. All that was left was his genuine and holy sorrow at the apostate condition of God's own people. That is why Elijah gave the same answer, because it was—largely—true. He was mistaken in saying he was the only one left, but otherwise the sorry picture he painted was all too accurate.

As we have seen in chapter three, there can be a depression which is holy. We *should* sorrow at sin (our own most of all), at suffering, injustice, cruelty, war, abortion, divorce, death, and all the other things that sin has brought into God's perfect world. I suspect that if you or I have a fresh and deep encounter with the God of the Bible we will sorrow *more,* not less. The Son of God became the "Man of Sorrows", and said, "Blessed are those who mourn." We will weep over Jerusalem—or Washington, or London—as Jesus did and does. And we will sorrow over the poor state of the people of God in so many places today.

Please don't misunderstand me. I do not mean that we will be introspective, morbid, and without hope. Our hope is in God. Sin, sorrow, and apostasy will not have the last word: not in the Church, not in Israel, not even in the world. And this leads to our final point:

6. A NEW ASSIGNMENT

The Lord said to him, "Go back the way you came, and go to the Desert of Damascus. When you get there, anoint Hazael king over Aram. Also, anoint Jehu son of Nimshi king over Israel, and anoint Elisha son of Shaphat from Abel Meholah to succeed you as prophet. Jehu will put to death any who escape the sword of Hazael, and Elisha will put to death any who escape the sword of Jehu. Yet I reserve seven thousand in Israel—all whose knees have not bowed down to Baal and all whose mouths have not kissed him."

(1 Kings 19:15-18)

Even now the Lord does not pat him on the back, congratulate him for his zeal, or commiserate with him on the state of things. Neither does God dismiss Elijah from his service. As we have seen, when Elijah emerged from the cave he covered his face with his cloak: in the old version, "his mantle". It was the symbol of his office, his calling as a prophet of God. Perhaps Elijah wondered if the Lord would now defrock him, tear the mantle from his hands, and tell him his call had been rescinded.

Oh no: *he sends him back with a new list of jobs to do.*

Do you remember what we said in an earlier chapter? Jesus came to show us the heart of God—what God is really like—and Jesus said, "A bruised reed he will not break, and a smoldering wick he will not snuff out" (Matthew 12:20). No, he does not cast aside his weary and wounded servants. He is a God full of grace. Keep that mantle, Elijah. I have further work for you.

If God does not call us to heaven, it is because he has work for us. We never retire—at least not until we get to heaven and enter into our rest. We are saved to serve. The sphere and nature of our service may be changed—or it may not. Elijah had to go right back where he came from.

Is that the word of the Lord to you? "Go back the way you came." You might have preferred to start again in a new place, with different people. But your commitment to serve the Lord is, "any time, any place, at any cost." So, if he tells you, "Go back," then back you will go! If you left your post through fear, exhaustion, or disappointment, God understands. He does not condemn you. He wants you to come to him and pour out your heart to him as Elijah did. In fact, he will use the entire experience to give you a new and fresh encounter with himself—but then he may well send you back! Back to that pulpit; back to that office; back to those

106

children ... wherever he has called you to serve. It may be difficult, but you know the Lord will be with you.

It does not serve our purpose to get involved in the details of Elijah's new assignments, but let me point out three things.

First, notice how God is in total and sovereign control and is instructing Elijah with regard to the political succession. It is the Lord who "sets up kings and deposes them" (Daniel 2:21). Some might imagine that God is only sovereign over the church and concerned only with prophets and priests. Oh no. He is concerned with kings and presidents, prime ministers and governments. He is sovereign ruler over all. Empires collapse at his word and worldly rulers owe their power entirely to his will and purpose. They serve only as a temporary scaffold around which God is building the eternal kingdom of his Son.

Second, notice how God is making provision for Elijah's succession. Elijah prayed to die, but his time was not yet. Nevertheless, one day he would indeed complete his earthly service and then be called home.

And then what? God always has another and another. No prophet is indispensable. Elijah's successor, Elisha, was already chosen out by God—though he was not yet aware of it. How lovely that Elijah is to have a young friend, a devoted servant, and an eager apprentice. Together they would do great things.

Third, see how God has to correct Elijah's perception in another way. Elijah thought he was the only one left who was faithful to the Lord. Oh no. Quite wrong! The sovereign Lord has "reserved" seven thousand who have not succumbed to the fashionable idolatry of Baalism. Perhaps Elijah thought he knew everything about God's cause. That is why he was so downcast and pessimistic. But he was wrong. There were seven thousand faithful ones, kept by God's electing grace, who Elijah did not even know about.

Things are not always what they seem. Are you depressed by what you see? But you don't see everything. Let us be true to ourselves and our own call and leave the rest to him whose kingdom has no end. Not all the Jezebels that hell can muster can extinguish the light of the gospel or thwart the onward, triumphant march of the kingdom of God.

CONCLUSION

So Elijah went from there and found Elisha, son of Shaphat..."

(1 Kings 19:19)

...And they went and founded bible colleges for the training of prophets loyal to the Lord. As for Ahab and Jezebel, from whom Elijah had fled, they both died violently and ignominiously. Elijah, however, whom they had despised and sought to destroy, after evening years of faithfulness and fruitfulness, was carried to heaven in triumph and a chariot of fire.

Why are you downcast, O my soul? Why so disturbed within me? Put your hope in God, for I will yet praise him, my Savior and my God.

(Psalm 42:5)

CHAPTER SIX

Doubt

AM I RIGHT TO TRUST IN JESUS?

When John heard in prison what Christ was doing, he sent his disciples to ask him, "*Are you the One who is to come, or should we expect someone else?*"

(Matthew 11:2)

D o you ever have doubts? Do you ever wonder if you are wasting your life trusting in Jesus?

A young man once asked me, "How do you know that you are not backing the wrong horse?" I had never quite heard Christianity put that way, but I knew what he meant. I tried to explain to him that I had asked that same question in different forms many times. How do I know that Christianity is the only true religion? How can I be so sure that Jesus Christ is the only way to heaven? If I had been born in some other part of the world, wouldn't I be a Buddhist, or a Muslim, or something else? How do I know that I am not backing the wrong horse? Good question.

If you are an unbeliever, you do well to ask that question. You want to know. At least, I hope you do, because it is the most important investigation you will ever make. I believe with all my heart your eternal destiny hangs upon the answer to this question.

But it may be that even *as a believer* you sometimes have doubts. Perhaps, during a time of difficulty or darkness, you begin to reflect, "You know, I have never seen God. In fact, I have never actually seen Jesus or even an angel. I wonder if it is all true. People talk about, 'God said this. God said that. God said such and such to me. God led me thus.' But what do they mean?"

You say to yourself, "I have never heard an audible voice. I wonder if I am really being a fool, giving up all this time to religion and giving up this talent that I have, to serve Jesus Christ. Maybe he's dead and gone like other religious leaders and I am just wasting my life. And, come to think of it, my money; my hard-earned meager resources! Should I really be giving so sacrificially to my church and to other Christian work? What if I am wasting it? I can think of a few other things to do with that money!"

Or perhaps you have been influenced by the fashions of today. In some circles, at any rate, it is very unfashionable to have strongly held beliefs. Certainty is out, doubt is in. Religion is acceptable only so long as you do not believe that certain things are true, and their opposites are false; that certain behavior is right, and its opposite is wrong; and that you keep your beliefs private. Perhaps you have been called "arrogant," "intolerant," "dogmatic," "extreme," or worse. Such designations can be disturbing.

You are not the only person who has been troubled by doubts, Christian friend. This chapter is primarily written for believers, or those who have professed belief but are now having doubts. That is why I will quote scripture frequently and base this study on the experience of a great believer—John the Baptist. Of all people, John experienced doubts about Jesus. (If you want to read about John you can do so in: Luke 1:5-25, 39-45, 57-80; Luke 3:1-20; Matthew 14:1-12; and John 1:19-35.) We will concentrate on the incident recorded in Matthew 11, verses 2-6, though I will refer to other incidents and statements during the course of this study.

When John heard in prison what Christ was doing, he sent his disciples to ask him, "Are you the One who is to come, or should we expect someone else?" Jesus replied, "Go back and report to John what you hear and see: The blind receive sight, the lame walk, those who have leprosy are cured, the deaf hear, the dead are raised, and the good news is preached to the poor. Blessed is the man who does not fall away on account of me."

(Matthew 11:2-6)

Now it is very surprising to find John having to ask this question. After all, John was a great prophet. Jesus said so. As a matter of fact, in this very chapter, verse 11, Jesus says: "I tell you the truth: Among those born of women there has not arisen anyone greater than John the Baptist."

It is also surprising because John *knew* that Jesus was the One.

He knew from a child. His father was a priest and his mother, Elizabeth, was the cousin of Mary, the mother of Jesus. In a very remarkable statement we are told in the Bible how Mary, when she had just conceived the child Jesus, went to see her cousin Elizabeth down in Judea. Elizabeth was six months into her pregnancy with John. When the two women met, the child in Elizabeth's womb, John, leapt for joy at the proximity of the Savior. We then read:

Elizabeth was filled with the Holy Spirit. In a loud voice she exclaimed: "Blessed are you among women, and blessed is the child you will bear! But why am I so favored, that the mother of my Lord should come to me?"

(Luke 1:41, 42)

I am sure you will agree with me, therefore, that from a child John must have been aware of some of the remarkable prophecies concerning both himself and his cousin.

He knew in the desert. John grew up to become a wilderness preacher enjoying remarkable success. One important aspect of his message was to point to One who was to come of whom he was but the forerunner, preparing the way. When he saw Jesus he

111

pointed to him and said, "Look, the Lamb of God who takes away the sin of the world!" (John 1:29)

He knew in the water. John used to baptize those who repented of their sins in the river Jordan, hence his nickname, "the Baptist." Jesus came for baptism and John said, "I am not worthy even to untie your sandals. You should baptize me."

And Jesus said, "No. You baptize me. It is right."

And so John did, and we read that John "... saw the Spirit of God descending like a dove and lighting on him. And a voice from heaven said, 'This is my Son, whom I love; with him I am well pleased'" (Matthew 3:16).

John had been told, "The man on whom you see the Spirit come down and remain is he ... I have seen and I testify that this is the Son of God" (John 1:33-34).

So how could John of all people have doubts since he knew who Jesus was from a child, and as a preacher, and when he baptized Jesus? I don't suppose you have had such amazing things happen to you as happened to John. I certainly haven't. So if he, after all those confirming experiences, could be attacked with doubts, little wonder if some of us sometimes are. That is why I have chosen this passage for a brief study of "Doubt." We will consider it from this point of view. First of all: how doubts may have arisen in his mind, and how they can arise in ours. And then: how Jesus dealt with his doubts and how *we* should deal with ours.

We will examine our text very carefully and see if it casts light upon John's problem.

Doubts may have arisen because:

He was a man—"When John..."

Who was John? Well, it says in John 1, verse 6, "There was a *man* sent from God whose name was John." Not Superman. Not an angel. But a man—John. The Bible says that temptation is *"common to man"* (1 Corinthians 10:13). No man or woman can escape being tempted. It is not a sin to be tempted. It is not a sin for a doubt to come into your mind. It may very well come from within or be put there by the evil one. Doubt is one of Satan's favorite weapons.

We read in the Bible that from the very beginning he used doubt to attack those whom God had created.

Satan even came to Jesus when he tempted him in the wilderness and said, in effect, "*If* you are the Son of God..." I mean, are you sure? "...*if* you are, don't you think you ought to do something that will put it beyond any doubt, and prove it? *If you are* ... turn these stones into bread." So certainly the temptation to doubt is something that is common to man. Of course we are taught that we must resist temptation. If we give in to it, if we welcome it, then that becomes a sin. I have written this chapter to help you to resist the temptation to doubt the gospel.

He was a preacher

Who was John? He was a faithful and fearless preacher. As a matter of fact the reason why he was in prison when he sent this message is because of his faithful and courageous preaching. He had denounced the king, Herod Antipas, for his adultery. Herod had taken his brother, Philip's wife, and John had said that was unlawful. They put him in prison and, later, took his life. And so, here is the evil one attacking this brave preacher.

Satan does attack preachers, you know. He also goes after other strategic Christians who may be in positions of influence. You have always to remember that Satan is not omnipresent. God is everywhere, but Satan is not. He is a created being. Powerful, yes, but limited, and he roams "through the earth, and going back and forth in it" (Job 1:7). He "prowls around like a roaring lion looking for someone to devour" (1 Peter 5:8). He is not alone. He has some evil spirits at his command. But they are of limited number. I know of no scripture that tells us that demons can reproduce. So, therefore, he has to have a strategy. If you were the devil, wouldn't you have a strategy? With your limited resources, wouldn't you target those who were doing you the most damage? That is why he goes after preachers. That is why he goes after evangelists. If this were a study in spiritual warfare, I think I could prove to you from scripture that Satan hates faithful preachers more than any other group of people.

He also goes after people who witness for Jesus Christ, or who are seeking to win their friends or their family for Jesus Christ. He targets people who pray. He obviously targets missionaries, especially those (too few alas) who are in front-line evangelism and church planting.

Do you feel, sometimes, that *you* have been targeted? Maybe it is because you are a threat to Satan by your prayers, by your witness, or because you are a preacher or support a preacher. All God's soldiers are targets for the enemy, but especially his officers. Satan's array of subtle but powerful weapons includes discouragement, depression, loneliness, fatigue, division, diversion, sexual immorality, financial anxiety and/or dishonesty, jealousy, pride, egotism, and—as in this case—*doubt*. What an arsenal! How strong we need to be in the day of battle. And we do well to stay clear of Satan's traps. As Jesus taught us to pray, "Lead us not into temptation, but deliver us from the evil one" (Matthew 6:13).

He was in prison—"When John heard *in prison...*"

Not only was he a man and a preacher, but he was in prison. It is one thing to have great assurance when the crowds are there and when they are coming from north, south, east, and west, to hear you preach as they had with John in his great ministry, and when there are long lines of people waiting to be baptized in the River Jordan. No doubt he was on a "high." He believed that judgment was coming at any time with the Christ. He, John, was the forerunner to prepare the way, and then revival was coming following the judgment. At long last the day had dawned. Hallelujah!

Now it is all very different. He is alone and in prison. He is allowed occasional prison visits from some of his followers but that is all he has—*and doubts*. Satan is cruel. He takes advantage of difficult circumstances and attacks us when we are weak, when we are lonely, sick, or disappointed.

I can imagine John wondering, "Why has God allowed this? I was faithful. Why has God allowed me to be arrested and put in prison like this? Why, if Jesus is the One, if he is the Christ—the Deliverer—why does he not deliver me? They tell me he works

114

miracles. Why does he not come and work a miracle for me? They tell me he can heal at a word, at a distance. He doesn't even have to be there. Why doesn't he just say a word then and get me out of this prison?" I wonder if those thoughts came to him. I wonder if he pondered, "He must know I am allowed some visitors. But days go by, weeks go by, months go by, and he never comes."

I can imagine Satan putting these kinds of thoughts into his mind, can't you? "You would think he would come and see you, John, wouldn't you? If he cares for you, wouldn't he at least come and visit you? Is he the One who is to come, or should you expect someone else?"

Does doubt sometimes come to *your* mind because you wonder why God doesn't solve your problem? Have you ever secretly and quietly puzzled within yourself, "If God is God and almighty, why doesn't he use just a teeny bit of that power to get me out of this mess I am in? If I am his child, why doesn't he do something for me? Why doesn't he heal me? Why doesn't he find me a job? Why doesn't he give me a husband? Why doesn't he grant us a child? If Jesus loves me, why doesn't he at least *visit* me? I feel so alone. I don't sense his presence. Is Jesus the One who should come, or should I look for somebody else?"

His expectations were unrealized—"When John heard in prison
what Christ was doing..."

Jesus was not what John expected, or else why ask the question? I mean, he obviously was surprised by what he was hearing. You see, the Lord Jesus was a holy man. He was God's man. John had believed with all his heart that Jesus was so much more righteous than he that he was not fit to do the most menial, dirty job for him. That is why he used to say, "I am not fit to untie his sandals." That meant to untie them with all the dirt and the dung and the garbage of the streets on them, and then to wash his feet. John said he was not worthy even to do that. That is how much more holy Jesus was.

Now John's idea of a holy man and a righteous man was presumably reflected in the lifestyle that John himself lived. And how did he live? Well, he lived very, very simply, and very, very ascetically. He did not buy good clothes he just made his own with some camel skin and a leather girdle.

He did not buy the best food. In fact he ate only what he could find in the little crevices and on the land. He was very thin. He believed that self-denial was the holy life. He probably expected that as a holy man also, Jesus would live the same way.

But Jesus was not like John. Jesus wore a beautiful seamless robe. It was a gift. It was like a custom made suit. Beautiful. Jesus went to dinner parties. He had some rich friends. He lived sometimes in the "Jerusalem set." Though many of Jesus' friends were from the poor, it was not exclusively so. A very high born and rich man named Joseph of Arimathea was his friend. Jesus did not live the same kind of lifestyle as John.

By the way, the differences between Jesus and John show us, do they not, that the holy life is not to be assessed in some stereotypical way. Don't judge your brother or your sister because they do not choose to express their Christianity, their holiness and their walk with the Lord just exactly as you express yours.

He relied upon reports—"When John _heard_..."

John had not been able to see Jesus for himself, of course, for quite a while. I imagine him asking these reporters (whom I suspect to have been prejudiced against Jesus), "But isn't Jesus a friend of the poor as well as the rich?"

"The poor? You could say that, John. Drunkards. He is a friend of those. Criminals. Tax collectors. Traitors. He is a friend of those. Prostitutes. He is a friend of those. The riff-raff. The scum. There are always a lot of women around. You know, people are talking, John. There's a woman called Mary Magdalene. We don't know if you know about her past history, but she is always hanging about. And the latest story is something about a woman in Samaria of all things; a notoriously immoral woman. Yes, you could say he is a friend of the poor. He is just not like you, John. Nothing like you at all."

"But doesn't he do miracles?"

"John, have you heard about his first miracle? He turned water into wine."

"You mean he turned wine into water."

"No. He turned water into wine. As a good Baptist preacher you would have done it the other way round John, we know that. You never touched a drop. But this is what he did, water into *wine*. And, what is more, one hundred and fifty gallons of it!"

If the Jesus, the "king" was not what John expected, neither was his "kingdom". You see, before John was imprisoned he had preached and predicted judgment.

> "The axe is already at the root of the trees, and every tree that does not produce good fruit will be cut down and thrown into the fire. I baptize you with water for repentance. But after me will come One who is more powerful than I, whose sandals I am not fit to carry. He will baptize you with the Holy Spirit and with fire. His winnowing fork is in his hand, and he will clear his threshing floor, gathering his wheat into the barn and burning up the chaff with unquenchable fire." Then Jesus came from Galilee.
>
> (Matthew 3:10-12)

But judgment had not come, and the bad people just went from bad to worse, like the evil king who had put him into prison. And revival had not come either. Yes, Jesus had a few disciples, but they were very few and, by all accounts, a very unlikely lot.

I wonder if your doubts come from the fact that things are not what you expected. Could it be that both the king and his kingdom have failed to fulfill *your* expectations? What did they tell you? Come forward to receive Christ and then what? If you make this decision you will never have another problem, you will never have another bad day. You will never have another difficulty. You will never be pressed again. You will never be lonely again. He will put a smile on your face, a spring in your step, and joy in your heart. Why it will be like getting high, except that you will be high on Jesus all the way to heaven. Is that what they told you?

And it has not been like that, has it, at least not all the time. Oh, it was wonderful at first, but then... Did they never tell you anything about a life of repentance, about a life of discipleship and discipline? Did they tell you about carrying a cross? Did no-one teach you about spiritual warfare? I am not surprised. I have been amazed how many Christians have no idea that we are soldiers engaged in a fierce battle with unseen enemies. Did they promise heaven *now*, when in fact heaven is *then*? Have things not turned out as you expected? The bad people still prosper, don't they, sometimes at any rate. The true church can seem so small. You might be the only Christian in your school, your office, or your family.

So these doubts come. You are not the only one. Many of us have trodden this path. Let me stress again: it is not a sin to be tempted with doubt. The crucial thing—as with any temptation—is, are we looking for a way forward to victory? How do we deal with doubt?

THE ANSWER

Let us move on, then, to the answer. What did Jesus reply? How can John be reassured?

> Jesus replied, "Go back and report to John what you hear and see: the blind receive sight, the lame walk, those who have leprosy are cured, the deaf hear, the dead are raised, and the good news is preached to the poor."
>
> (Matthew 11:4-6)

Obviously there is only one way to answer doubts, and that is to come back to the person and work of Jesus Christ. We will not find an answer by looking at the church. The church is a company of sinners saved by grace. When I am tempted to doubt, looking at the church usually gives me more doubts! We will not find an answer to our doubts by looking at ourselves—that, too, will make it worse! We will not find an answer to our doubts by engaging in long, philosophical arguments. There is only one place to come and that is to Jesus—where we came in the first place—and look again at the Savior. We must examine again his life, his teaching, his miracles, his death, and his resurrection. In other words: back to the Gospels. We must spend a long time with Jesus. We must soak ourselves in the Gospels.

Jesus replied, "Go back and report to John what you hear and see." What did they hear and see? What will you and I hear and see if we read one or more of the Gospels?

His Mighty Deeds

This is what we see:

> "The blind receive sight, the lame walk, those who have leprosy are cured, the deaf hear, the dead are raised."
>
> (Matthew 11:4)

The Bible says these mighty works of Christ were *signs*. Signposts. The Apostle John wrote this at the end of his Gospel:

> Jesus did many other miraculous signs in the presence of his disciples, which are not recorded in this book. But these are written that you may believe that Jesus is the Christ, the Son of God, and that by believing you may have life in His name.
>
> (John 20:30-31)

These miracle cures cannot easily be explained away. I know that there is such a thing as psychosomatic healing. I know that some of us have complaints and symptoms that may be more in the mind than the body, and that if only we could find the trigger we would get over it, we would be cured. I know that. It is, however, very difficult to explain Jesus' ministry that way—as if it was some kind of hypnosis. For one thing, the people he healed he healed *instantly*. It was not some slow recovery. They did not turn the corner then gradually get better due to a new attitude or renewed hope. Instantly at his word and at his touch they were healed.

He healed, sometimes, *distantly*. He was not even there. He gave the word, and the people went home and discovered their friend or loved one healed. The Lord Jesus healed *perfectly*. He had a one hundred percent success rate, in the sense that all those that he pronounced whole were whole. No long disappointed lines of crestfallen people who had gone forward for healing and were not healed. When you read the Gospels, and you read the healing ministry of our Lord Jesus Christ, you are in a very different world from these so-called "Healing Ministries" that we see on our televisions today.

And he healed *creatively*. A man with a withered arm, all the sinews gone away, atrophied, diseased. Not only was he given the power back, but all the muscles and the sinews and the nerves were instantly renewed. There was a man who was a paralytic for thirty eight years. He had never walked. Now any doctor would tell you that even if his paralysis was only in his mind—and that is hard to believe—after all that time his body would be unable to walk. Yet he got up from his bed and, having rolled up his mattress, went out praising God.

When the misguided disciples in the Garden of Gethsemane struck at Malchus, one of the soldiers come to arrest Jesus, and cut off his ear, Jesus reached out and created a new ear. The blind that he healed were not short-sighted. They were *blind*. The lame were not just some who had been discovered to have one leg slightly shorter than the other. These were paralytics who could not walk and in some cases had never walked. Lepers were the untouchables and the incurables. Jesus touched them and healed them. The deaf were not the hard of hearing. They were deaf and often dumb as well.

As these emissaries of John went around and observed the Lord Jesus' ministry, they even saw him raise the dead. Not many of the modern day healers are to be found in the cemeteries and the mortuaries, are they? But Jesus was there. His enemies could not gainsay it. They said that he did it by demonic power.

If you read the Gospels you will read how he stilled the storm, so that even experienced fishermen and sailors marveled at his control of the waves as well as the winds. Storms may die down suddenly but the waves are disturbed for a long time afterwards. Jesus stilled *both* at his command. You will read how he fed the multitude; how he walked on water; how he died and on the third day rose triumphant from the grave. The resurrection is especially important. If you accept the invitation of Jesus and walk around with him, observing his ministry, you will see his mighty deeds.

His Gracious Words

"Go back and report to John what you hear ... and the good news is preached to the poor."

(Matthew 11:4-5)

You will also hear something: his gracious message. "Never man spoke like this man," they said. People were astonished at his teaching—see Matthew 7:28-29; John 7:46. Even many unbelievers today say that Jesus had the highest ethical teaching that the world has ever heard.

Why does he mention the poor? Because all other ways of getting right with God favor the rich. How much can you pay? How many offerings can you bring? What contributions can you make? How many penances can you do? How many pilgrimages can you fit in? How many good works can you accomplish? To how many charities can you contribute? How many of this? How much of that? But you never know if you have done enough. The gospel of Jesus Christ says there is *nothing* you can do. He has paid it all. "And the good news is preached to the poor." If anything for once the rich are disadvantaged because they tend to be mesmerized by their riches.

The eighteenth century hymn writer Joseph Hart wrote these words:

Come, ye sinners, poor and needy, Weak and wounded, sick and sore;
Jesus ready stands to save you, Full of pity, love, and power.
He is able. He is able. He is willing; doubt no more.

I remember going to Joseph Hart's tomb in Bunhill Fields, just off the City Road, London, and being deeply moved just to see the inscription:

Oh, bring no purse God's grace is free;
To Paul, to Magdalene, to me.

"Come to me," said Jesus, "all you who are weary and burdened, and I will give you rest" (Matthew 11:28). Has anyone ever uttered such a gracious message as fell from Jesus' lips? I can say, as one who has spent fifty years proclaiming this good news; whoever you are, whatever you have done, however low you have sunk, the Savior invites you, "Come to me." What about your sins? He died for our sins. It was for that he came. "And the blood of Jesus, his Son, purifies us from all sin" (1 John 1:7). Some people will never forgive your bad deeds. Some will say they forgive but they will never forget. He both forgives *and* forgets. Your sins are *gone*. And if you come to him according to his gracious invitation, he will receive you and accept you. He will write your name in his Book of Life, and take you home to heaven when you die. He will love you *forever*.

Has anyone ever brought to the world such a message?

His Unique Person

In a way, Jesus replied to this delegation that had come from John (and these must have been faithful emissaries who would report accurately), "Stay for a while. Just come around with us and see what I do. Listen to what I say. Watch me and *get to know me*. Then go back to John and just tell him what you have observed."

In his reply to John, Jesus quotes from Isaiah 35:5-6 and 61:1-2. John knew his Bible and in this way Jesus is indirectly telling him that he is indeed the One of whom the scriptures prophesy.

As you and I carefully read the Gospels—and in one sense the whole Bible—we are not only seeing what Jesus did and hearing what Jesus taught, but we are *meeting him*. I think it is the only way for any of us. You see, Jesus was indeed very different from John, but he is not to be judged by someone else's standard. He *is* the standard. John must not judge Jesus. That's what Jesus means in verse 6, "Blessed is the man who does not fall away on account of me."

Peter says, "There was no deceit in him." Paul says, "He knew no sin." The centurion said, "Surely this was a righteous man, the Son of God." Even Pontius Pilate—the cowardly, cruel Pontius Pilate—said, "I find no fault in him."

Of course, you will read the things he said about himself; all the declarations that he made concerning his own Person. Some unbelievers say, "Oh, yes, he is the greatest. His is the highest ethical teaching we have ever heard. The Sermon on the Mount is the very best. But he was not divine. He was not the Son of God." But they cannot just pick out the ethics and the parables and the Sermon on the Mount and reject the things Jesus said concerning himself.

Just imagine with me, if you would, if some person with presidential aspirations in America today, some hopeful who seemed to come from nowhere, was taken aside by the press who said, "Where did you come from?"

And he replied, "I came from heaven. The Father who sent me, sent me to you."

"Really! Well, who are you?"

"I am the light of the world. He who comes to me will never walk in darkness. I am the bread of life. He who feeds on me will never hunger. He who drinks of the water that I give him will never thirst. I am the resurrection and the life, he who believes in me, though he die yet will he live, and whoever lives in me will never die."

And the reporters say, "Do you think you are God?"

And he says, "He who has seen me has seen the Father. I and my Father are one. And one day all the nations of the earth will gather before me and I will judge them."

They would say, "This man is a megalomaniac. He is mentally deranged. He needs treatment. He needs medication. He needs a psychiatrist."

Mind you, perhaps if he had just been down to the local hospital and touched all the beds in the Cancer Care Unit and everybody had got up and gone home healed, they might take him seriously. If he had just been down to where all the AIDS patients were dying, and at a word they had been completely made whole, these reporters might hesitate before dismissing him. If he had been walking up Main Street and a funeral cortege came and he stopped it and there was a poor widow crying her eyes out, and he said, "What has happened?" And she said, "My boy, my only son, has just been shot in a drug gang killing." And he said to her, "Don't cry. Wipe your tears." And the boy got up out of the casket and was made well. What would the press think then? That is what Jesus did.

Yes, perhaps then the press would take him seriously. Do you take him seriously? Who is this man, Jesus? Was he mad? Do *you* think he should have been put away in a psychiatric hospital? What, this man of compassion: this man of love, who reached out to children, and to widows and orphans, and the incurables, and the outcasts, and the "don't-come-near-us" lepers? Mad? The preacher of the Sermon on the Mount, the Golden Rule, and all the other wonderful things Jesus taught? He always seems to me to have been the sanest man who ever lived.

Bad! Was he bad? Did he know that he was none of the things that he declared himself to be, but he was just trying to fool gullible people to get followers. Was he trying to make money out of innocent people? Was he a bad man? Or was it all those disciples who were bad? Did they invent all these stories about Jesus?

Sometimes I have been asked, "Harry, is it possible these are all myths and legends?"

I have rejected that theory. I have only space to say that Peter, James, John, and company were not evil liars—not to mention Jesus' mother, Mary. Furthermore, they would not have been willing to die as martyrs for a "life" that was a total fiction. No-one could invent Jesus. Anyway, what about the resurrection of Jesus? I am one-hundred-percent convinced of the historical fact of the resurrection—and I have examined all the alternative explanations very carefully. I believe with all my heart: Jesus died, Jesus rose from the dead, and Jesus is alive today and for ever.

So, if he wasn't mad, and if he wasn't bad, and if he isn't fiction, then isn't he God? Don't you see that when we have these doubts it is no use trying to resolve them with philosophical arguments? Intellectual discussions on important topics have their place, but, speaking for myself, they are not the way to handle serious attacks of doubt. No, the only way to handle those is to come right back to Jesus. Going round and round with arguments won't cut it.

Let me say again: it is no use looking at the church. We will only get worse. Our doubts will not be resolved if we focus on the preacher. He too, like you and me, is but a sinner saved by grace. There he is, like John, weak and weary, fighting on the front line, standing in the need of prayer.

We must not look inward at ourselves. For most of us that is worst of all! We are dismayed at our own sinfulness. There is only one place to look, and that is at *him*. "Turn your eyes upon Jesus."

A Christian is not someone who thinks the church is perfect, or who has been convinced only that the world did not make itself, and therefore there must be a God. The devil believes in God! A Christian is a person who has found Jesus, and who has decided that there is no other way to explain this life. Jesus is the One, and I do not need to look anywhere else, and I give my heart and my life to him.

Have you ever read one of the Gospels at one sitting? You can read Mark's Gospel in one hour; John's in two. Is not your eternal soul worth that time and effort? Meet Jesus. What do you think concerning him? Who is he? Do you put him with a list of "greats"? Socrates, Alexander, Mohammed, Washington, Lincoln, Churchill, Gandhi, Jesus. Is that where he belongs?

Or, do you not believe as I do that he towers alone above all other men and women? Not, "Jesus the *Great*," but, "Jesus the *Only*"—the eternal Son of God, the King of Kings and Lord of Lords.

If you have never done so, will you trust in Jesus today? If you have done so, but sometimes doubts come upon you, trust him all over again. Resist the devil and defeat him.

Friend, Jesus never said that being a believer would be easy. There are things we do not understand now which will be revealed hereafter. But he loves you. He died for you. He has a life for you to live, and a work for you to do. He will never leave you or forsake you. Let us resist the spirit of the age to center wholly upon ourselves. Let us instead, *"fix our eyes on Jesus, the author and perfecter of our faith"* (Hebrews 12:2).

Not only is this the way to deal with doubt. You will be surprised how many other problems are solved in precisely the same way.

Finally—and this is very important—the antidote to doubt is not only to look again at Jesus and acknowledge him to be *the* Lord. I must kneel at his feet and surrender to him as *my* Lord. Will you say to him, with me, "Lord Jesus, I yield to you complete sovereign rights over every aspect of my life. I want you to make of this mixed-up, weak, sinful, human soul, a person more and more like you; whatever it takes to do it. I want you to fill my heart with your love and use me in your kingdom in whatever capacity you choose. In short, I want to live only for the glory of my Savior whom I love so dearly, who first loved me and gave himself for me. Life is but a vapor and mine will soon be over. You are preparing a place for me in heaven. When you call me home, I want to hear you say, notwithstanding my many failures, 'Welcome home, and well done!'"

> Jesus! the name high over all, In hell, or earth, or sky;
> Angels and men before it fall, And devils fear and fly.
>
> Oh that the world might taste and see the riches of his grace;
> The arms of love that compass me would all mankind embrace.
>
> His only righteousness I show, His saving grace proclaim;
> 'Tis all my business here below to cry: "Behold the Lamb!"
>
> Happy, if with my latest breath I might but gasp his name;
> Preach him to all, and cry in death: "Behold, behold the Lamb!"
>
> —Charles Wesley

CHAPTER SEVEN

Anguish

MY GOD, WHY...?

From the sixth hour until the ninth hour darkness came over all the land. About the ninth hour Jesus cried out in a loud voice, "Eloi, eloi, lama sabachthani?"—which means, "*My God, my God, why* have you forsaken me?"

(Matthew 27:45-46)

In Jerusalem, at the time of the year called "Passover," the midday sun beats down relentlessly, encouraging travelers to find whatever relief they can in the shade. On the day when Jesus died, however, it was different. At twelve noon, the skies went as dark as midnight and remained that way for three hours. About 150 years later, the Christian apologist, Tertullian, pleading the cause of Christ and his church to a persecuting Roman government wrote, "Look in your own archives and you will see that it was recorded there was a strange darkness at midday for three hours at the time when this man died in Judea."

Deep darkness just seemed to wrap round this fourth cry of our Lord from the cross, "My God, my God, why have you forsaken me?" But is it any wonder the sun refused to shine? Surely this was the most anguished, agonized, mysterious, cry in the whole of human history. It is also—as we shall see—the cry most pregnant with meaning: a cry, not only with pain, but with grace and with hope.

What do we hear in this cry?

THERE IS ANGUISH IN THIS CRY

"My God, why...?" How often has that bewildered cry been wrung from the lips of the sufferer?

Why has my loved one been taken?

Why have I lost my child?

Why have my hopes and dreams been dashed?

Why is my body racked day after day, and night after night, with unrelieved pain?

Why is my heart broken with unrequited love?

My God, *why*?

Maybe someone reading this chapter is asking this very question right now. There seems to be neither end nor purpose to your suffering. You cry out to God, either because you cannot understand how a God of infinite love can permit this for one of his children or because, since he alone knows the reason why he would do so, you also would like to know. Certainly you can find no reason yourself. Like Jesus, whose anguished cry pierced the darkness, so does yours. You cannot help it. My God, *why*?

"Forsaken"—what a meaningful, heart-rending, anguish word this is. To be forsaken, abandoned, cast off, deserted, is always hurtful; to be forsaken of God is worst of all. This cry has been called, "The Cry of Dereliction."

Children, sometimes, are forsaken by their parents. Parents are sometimes forsaken by their children. Maybe in their sunset years, just when they need the children most—to call, to write, to visit—they are cruelly abandoned. It is heartbreaking. Friend sometimes forsakes friend. Most of Jesus' friends forsook him at the end. Wives are being increasingly forsaken by husbands and husbands by wives. The Bible speaks about the fact that the church should always be a haven and a loving source of grace to widows and orphans. The widows and orphans of today include those women and children who have been abandoned. They also cry.

Physical pain is hard to bear, but there are pains of the heart that are worse and misery of the soul beyond endurance.

The Lord Jesus uttered no cry of anguish when they nailed his tender flesh to the cross. Instead he prayed, "Father, forgive them." He uttered no cry of pain as he gasped in agony with every breath. Instead he had words of hope and assurance for the penitent criminal suffering beside him. Jesus was silent when his tormenters walked by and mocked him. When he did speak it was to make provision for his mother, committing her to the care of his most beloved disciple.

At last, however, after six hours an anguished cry is rent from his lips. What is it? It is not, "Why did Judas betray me?" It is not, "Why did Peter deny me?" He does not cry, "Why, oh why, did my disciples desert me?" No doubt those things hurt him deeply. But this was the worst by far, "My God, my God, why have *you* forsaken me?"

Oh, what anguish of soul when love is severed! If you love someone deeply, even temporary parting is painful. That is why we see the soldier's wife weeping at the army base or the widow weeping at the grave. It is worse when love is replaced by misunderstanding or by anger. Where once there had been such oneness, love, and joy, now a cloud has come. There is a rift, a gulf. The deeper the love and the closer the bond, the worse the pain when something threatens to destroy it.

And that is one aspect of what the Lord Jesus was going through, for there had never been a love, either before or since, like the love of the Son for the Father, and the Father for the Son. It was a perfect love. It was and is eternal. All other loves that we might have are but a pale reflection of the intensity, the union, and the oneness of the love of the Father for the Son. Yet here on the cross, Jesus is undergoing the awful anguish of separation when God replaces love with wrath.

C.H. Spurgeon said, "I do not think that the records of time or even of eternity contain a sentence more full of anguish … Here you may look as if into a vast abyss, and though you strain your eyes and gaze until sight fails you, yet you perceive no bottom. It is measureless, unfathomable, inconceivable, this anguish of the Savior on your behalf and mine. It is no more to be measured and weighed than the sin which needed it, or the love which endured it. We will adore where we cannot comprehend."

Yes: we hear anguish in this cry.

THERE IS MYSTERY IN THIS CRY

Whenever has a righteous man or a woman, I ask, been deserted of God at the point of death? It is usually the very opposite. When we read our biographies, history books, and testimonies, the godly man or woman finds God very faithful and close at the moment of dying. David said, "Even though I walk through the valley of the shadow of death, I will fear no evil: for you are with me; your rod and your staff, they comfort me" (Psalm 23:4). No dereliction there.

The apostle Paul, writing to Timothy from prison while facing death, writes in heartrending words of being deserted by almost everyone. But then he says, "... the Lord stood at my side and gave me strength" (2 Timothy 4:17).

So has been the experience of saints and martyrs when they have come to the end of the journey. The Lord has stood by them and given them strength and, sometimes, even more radiance at the stake or in the arena or before the executioner than at any other time. Like Stephen of old they see the doors to heaven opened and the Lord waiting to carry them home to their reward. As they come to the river, on the other side they glimpse the glory.

One of my most vivid childhood memories is an event which happened a few days before the death of my mother when I was seven years old. She had contracted rheumatic fever when she was a child that led to heart valve disease in adult life. I hardly remember her as anything but an invalid who for the last years of her life was confined to bed.

One day from her bed in a ground-floor room, she called my father's name, "Jim, Jim." There was such an unexpected strength and excitement in her voice that not only did my father rush to her side, but my grandmother and I entered the room also. I distinctly recall that my mother was sitting up in bed and leaning forward away from her piled-up pillows. She appeared to be gazing upward and had a radiant look on her face which I had never before seen, or ever since forgotten.

"What is it, dear?" asked my father. "What is it?"

"Oh Jim," she said—not looking at him but continuing to gaze upward with such intensity that I looked upward also—"Oh Jim, I have just seen Jesus."

"Have you, my dear? What was he like?"

"Oh Jim," my mother replied, "he was all shining and his arms were outstretched towards me."

I think some more questions were asked of her but my father and grandmother were crying and I was taken from the room. A few days later my mother went to heaven to those welcoming arms.

My mother was not forsaken, quite the reverse. On her death bed the Lord in his tenderness made his presence known to her in this remarkable way.

As a pastor I have been privileged to visit with other saints of the Lord who have known that special presence in their last hours. So much so that, though I confess to be afraid of pain, I am not afraid to die. I know my Lord will not forsake me. He will be there when the time comes.

But not so with the Lord Jesus. Yet Jesus was the most righteous man who ever lived, the only human being who could truly say, "I always do the will of my Father." Nevertheless he was apparently forsaken in his most severe moment of need; seemingly abandoned at his hour of death. So he thought, and so he declared.

Perhaps you think he was mistaken. Perhaps you think his mind was confused, damaged by his dreadful injuries and suffering. This sometimes happens such that the person speaks out of character and we say, "He is not himself." There is a very close interdependency between body, mind, and spirit. When someone is severely ill other aspects of their human nature can be adversely affected. When faced with their groans and utterances we must make due allowance. They are not responsible. They say things they would not otherwise say or believe. Is this the explanation for this mystery? Was Jesus mistaken? Had his mind collapsed? I do not believe so. He had refused a proffered drink because it contained some anesthetic. He would have his mind kept clear. No, he was not mistaken, for reasons we will consider.

Or do you believe this was just the cry of a disillusioned man, a self-styled Messiah, who expected God to deliver him "in extremis." No, because Jesus had prophesied that he must die (Matthew 16:21). The cross was not unexpected. He had said he could call upon twelve legions of angels to save him but that the cross was his destiny (Matthew 26:52-54).

Or perhaps you think this was due to Satan's attack. Surely Satan, should he be permitted to do so, would attack a man or woman of God even in their dying hours? Satan has no mercy and is the very personification of vindictiveness. Add to that the fact that Satan hates Jesus Christ more than he has hated any other human being. Furthermore, Satan is the father of lies and will seek to persuade the believer that he is deserted of God even when no such desertion has taken place. All that is true. Satan is, and does, all those things and many more. Satan was undoubtedly at Golgotha that day—the betrayal, the desertion, the cruelty, the injustice, the mockery, and the murder prove that—but Satan is not the explanation for the Savior's agonized cry.

Jesus spoke the truth. Jesus of Nazareth, love incarnate, was indeed forsaken of God. What a mystery!

But there is another aspect to the mystery of this cry of dereliction. How can God be deserted by God? Is Jesus not God in the flesh? Does not the Gospel of John begin with these words, "In the beginning was the Word, and the Word was with God, and the Word was God ... The Word became flesh and made his dwelling among us" (John 1:1,14). Did not the Lord Jesus say in John 8:58, "Before Abraham was born, I AM!" The Jewish authorities rightly recognized that as a claim to deity, and took up stones to stone him, the penalty by law for blasphemy. Jesus said to his disciples, "Anyone who has seen me has seen the Father... I am in the Father, and the Father is in me" (John 14:9,11). "I and my Father are one" (John 10:30). The Apostle Paul wrote, "For in Christ all the fullness of the Deity lives in bodily form" (Colossians 2:9).

How then can God be deserted by God?

The great Reformer, Martin Luther, set himself to study this verse. He fasted. He spoke to no one for hours. He sat still, not moving, like as if he was in a trance. And then he began to walk around the room and he began to say, "God, forsaken of God. Who can understand that?"

No one can completely understand it. I think it relates to the fact that our Lord Jesus was two natures in one Person. Fully divine, yet fully human. And here he was, the man, Jesus of Nazareth, dying on the cross, forsaken of God.

By the way, do you know Jesus always addressed God as his Father except this one time. Even on the cross he prayed, "Father, forgive them." But during those three dark hours he addressed his Father as, "My God, my God..." Surely the ground on which we are standing is holy ground.

There is mystery in this cry.

THERE IS GRACE IN THIS CRY

Why? The Lord asks the question, "Why?" "My God, my God, why have you forsaken me?" We also want to know that. Why? Why must this beautiful life end like this? Why must these compassionate, healing hands be nailed to a cross like this? Why must the One who dwelt in love with the Father from all eternity be separated from that love? "Father, why did you forsake Jesus? Why did the sky go dark? What is taking place here? Will you explain it to us?"

Yes, God has explained it to us. His explanation is in the Bible. You could almost say that the Bible *is*, from beginning to end, God's explanation of the cross. The Bible is God's Word to mankind and its message centers on the cross. As we have said, there are some aspects of the cross which are beyond our understanding, but other aspects God has made as plain and simple as possible. More than anything, God wants all of us to understand the message of the cross and why Jesus, his Son, uttered this awful cry. Then, having heard the message, we must act upon it.

The Father's answer to you and me is, "You ask me, Why the cross? You want to know why my Son had to die. My Son came for you. He died for you. We were separated for you. Don't you realize that?'"

"For me, Father? Tell me how."

God, Man and Sin

God is *holy*. He cannot look upon sin. That does not mean that he does not know about it and see it, because God is omniscient and sees and knows everything. He is God. It means he can have no fellowship with sin. God is light, and sin is darkness, and in him there is no darkness at all. Because he is holy, God is revolted by sin and he must turn away from it.

Man is *sinful*. Sin is not some abstract thing. Sin is what sinners do and say and think. So the sinful things we do and say and think are offensive to him. Is that a strange concept? It shouldn't be. Even we are sometimes revolted by sin and angry with the sinner. Think of how you feel when faced with terrible cruelty—especially to a child—or the violence of an abusive husband who beats his wife, or ugly examples of greed or malice. Could anyone see the movie *Schindler's List*, or read about the Holocaust, and not be repulsed? Well if we, who ourselves are sinners, can experience the kind of revulsion we sometimes feel at the worst examples of human behavior, can we not begin to understand that God, who is pure light and holiness, is revolted by *all* sin—including yours and mine.

Not only that, but also God is *just* and must punish the sinner. He cannot merely turn away and ignore it. Is that also a strange concept? Again, it shouldn't be. Once more we see that reflected in ourselves. God, who is the source of all true justice, has made us in his image, and we desire that criminals be punished for their evil deeds. When a terrorist plants a bomb which kills innocent bystanders; when a little child is abducted, tortured, and murdered; when someone cheats elderly people of their life savings with tricks and lies; we do not say, "Oh dear, never mind, it doesn't matter."

Our whole being cries for justice. In fact, many believe that certain offenses deserve the death penalty.

Do you know that the Bible says that God pronounced the death penalty upon *all* sin? Not only murders—every sin—your sins and my sins. The Bible says that the soul that sins will die and, "The wages of sin is death" (Romans 6:23). It does not mean physical death only. It is referring to spiritual death and eternal death—the anguish of being shut out from the glorious and gracious presence of God for ever. The Bible speaks of it as "outer darkness." Shut out into darkness. God has appointed a Judgment Day.

The Meaning of the Cross

Here is the good news. God is not only holy and just he is also loving, kind, and full of grace. No sooner had sin entered the world but God promised a Savior. Do you remember how even in the Garden of Eden God came seeking, and God came calling? Adam and Eve had sought to hide from God and cover their shame with leaves—the first effort of man to try to deal with his sin in his own way and by his own efforts. But that wouldn't do. Having drawn them out to confess their sins, God graciously covered them with the skin of an animal which had been slain. God was showing them that if they were not to suffer the penalty of eternal death then "someone" must die in their place. But the death of a lamb or a kid was only a temporary expedient. It could not take away sin or satisfy the justice of God. God promised Eve that one day someone would be born of a woman who would do that—but only at tremendous cost to himself.

At last, after thousands of years of symbols and signs, prophecies and rituals, the Lord Jesus came and the promises were fulfilled. Calling attention to Jesus, John the Baptist cried, "Behold the Lamb of God who takes away the sins of the world." So Jesus went to die on the cross for us, condemned as if he were the worst sinner that ever lived.

Listen to the Scriptures:

We all, like sheep, have gone astray, each of us has turned to his own way; and the Lord has laid on him the iniquity of us all.
(Isaiah 53:6)

God made him who had no sin to be sin for us, so that in him we might become the righteousness of God.
(2 Corinthians 5:21)

Christ redeemed us from the curse of the law by becoming a curse for us.
(Galatians 3:13)

For Christ died for sins once for all ... to bring you to God
(1 Peter 3:18).

God looked upon his own beloved Son as if he were a murderer, an idolater, a blasphemer, a fornicator, a liar, a cheat, a hypocrite, and every other kind of sinner that a person can be. In his holiness God was revolted and turned away, and in his justice God was angry and smote his own Son. But we have said Jesus was a righteous man and a godly man? The only truly sinless man. Yes, Jesus died as our representative and substitute. This was all for us. Theologians call it "Substitutionary Atonement." It is the very heart of the Christian gospel. Hymn writers usually put it more simply:

Bearing shame and scoffing rude,
In my place condemned he stood;
Sealed my pardon with his blood:
Hallelujah! What a Savior!

—Philipp Bliss

And the darkness. What was the darkness? Nobody has ever been able to explain it. It cannot have been an eclipse of the sun, because Passover was always at full moon. Some have said it was nature protesting at what was taking place—the creation mourning the death of its Creator—for the hands nailed to the cross were the ones that fashioned the stars, and the voice now crying out in anguish was the same voice that in the beginning said, "Let there be light." No wonder the sun hid its face.

However, I believe it was more than that. It was because darkness is a symbol of sin. And darkness is a picture of judgment and eternity without God. So there was darkness for those three hours as Jesus hung on the cross because he went into outer darkness, bearing the darkness of night for sin, for you and me. Now, do you understand it?

Well might the sun in darkness hide,
And shut his glories in,
When Christ, the mighty Maker, died
For man the creature's sin.

—Isaac Watts

A Vital Question

Now the most important question of all: what have you done about it? This salvation which Christ bought for us on the cross is a gift that we must accept. The Bible says: "The wages of sin is death but the gift of God is eternal life" (Romans 6:23). Are you sure you have received this gift? Are you certain that you are saved? If you were to die tonight do you know, beyond any doubt, that you would go to heaven—not saved by something you have done but by receiving Jesus Christ?

Let me tell you a true story of Joan of Arc, the heroine of France. Born in 1412 in Domrémy, a little village on the River Meuse, she was the illiterate daughter of a ploughman. As a young girl she claimed to have visions that she should actually lead the French armies to victory against the English and the Burgundians, who had been at war with France for decades. It was called, "The Hundred Years War."

Of course at first people regarded her as slightly mad, but eventually she was taken to the pretender king, King Charles. He was impressed that she knew him notwithstanding his heavy disguise.

So, though only seventeen, she was given a suit of armor, a sword, and a battalion to lead. To the astonishment of all France she began to enjoy victory after victory. She even took the great city of Orléans. That is why she is always called the "Maid of Orléans." She was wounded but she bravely fought on until, in 1429, Charles was crowned king.

Later, intent upon trying to add to her successes, Joan was captured. She was tried by the English as a witch, was found guilty, and when that verdict was endorsed by the Paris ecclesiastical court, she was burned alive in the market place in Rouen. She was nineteen years old.

The French government wanted to do something to honor her memory. They discovered that the village from where she came, Domrémy, owed a tremendous debt of taxes, which they never could pay. Somebody was sent from the king who asked for the book which recorded all the inhabitants and the terrible debts they each owed. Then on each page it was written, "Debts remitted for the Maid's sake." Page after page, name after name, "Debts remitted for the Maid's sake."

In heaven there are also books? One for each of us. They too are full of debts, all the sins that we have committed. There is only this difference: some are awaiting the Judgment, while others have this written across them in red, "Debts remitted for the Son's sake."

What does it say on your book? If you are not sure—make sure. If you need further help write to me. It is not to do with being a Baptist, or a Presbyterian. It is not to do with being a Roman Catholic or a Protestant, Jew or Gentile. It is to do with being a sinner in the need of grace, and coming and saying, "Oh God, have mercy on me a sinner, for Christ's sake. I believe he died for me, was forsaken for me, and I trust in him and him alone as my Savior." Even though you pray that prayer in simple stumbling words, that is all that it requires. The moment you do that, written across the page are the words, "Sins all gone. Debts remitted for Jesus' sake."

You cannot pay for your sins. Some people think that by doing good deeds or going to church or giving money or keeping the Ten Commandments, their sins will be wiped out. Good though these things are, even though you did them all diligently and even perfectly (which nobody does or can), that could never erase even *one* sin. Only the blood of Christ can do that. If we could buy or earn our own salvation would Jesus have left heaven and died on the cross? Of course not. The cross was the only way. Jesus said. "I am the way and the truth and the life. No one comes to the Father except through me" (John 14:6).

Now I must tell you something more that I can hear.

THERE IS WARNING IN THIS CRY

What if you reject him? Does it matter? Indeed it does. My friend, if you are unsaved I would be an unfaithful messenger if I did not tell you that this cry of dereliction is the eternal cry of all those who have chosen to reject the Savior. The cry of hell is exactly this cry, "My God, my God, why have you forsaken me?" It is a cry that goes on day after day after day, night after night after night, on and on and on. If you die in your sins, that is what you will cry, with no escape. There is no road from hell to heaven.

I know we don't hear much about this nowadays. It is unfashionable. But the great question is not, is it fashionable or is it palatable, but is it true? If you doubt it I suggest you study Matthew 25:31-46, Luke 12:5, Luke 16:19-31, Revelation 20:10-15. I cannot avoid it. It horrifies me, but if it were not so, Jesus would never have needed to die. From what would he have needed to save us?

Do you know that our loving and tender Lord Jesus spoke more of hell than anyone else in the Bible? That is because he knows what it is like and he does not want anyone to go there. He does not want you to go there. That is why he died for you.

Some people have thought that Jesus went to hell after he died ("He descended into hell," says the Apostles Creed). Personally I do not believe that. I believe he went to heaven. I do think, however, that in a sense he went to hell *before* he died, because there on the cross he took all the punishment—the eternal, spiritual, awful punishment—for your sins and for mine. The cross tells us how much God hates sin, but also to what amazing lengths God has gone in love and grace to save the sinner.

The holiness, justice, love, and grace of God all meet at the cross.

THERE IS HOPE IN THIS CRY

It might seem strange to you that this cry, which appears on the surface so hope*less*, should give us hope. But so it is.

In our modern way of speaking, "hope" is a rather "if" kind of word. That is to say, it speaks of things that might or might not come to pass; we just "hope so". We say, "I hope it will be a nice day for our picnic," but we have no assurance whether it will be or not. Maybe it will rain. "Hope," in the Christian vocabulary is quite different. It is being certain of what you do not see and assured of the glory of what is yet to come.

Here are just four of the unseen certainties that hope brings to my heart when we come to the cross and hear this cry.

The Certain Hope of Sins Forgiven

Because Jesus paid the price for my sin—all of it—I will never have to pay. "Therefore, there is now no condemnation for those who are in Christ Jesus" (Romans 8:1). Sins past, present, and yes, even future have been covered by his blood.

The Certain Hope of his Compassion and Care

Always remember Jesus knows how you feel and what you are going through. He has been there. Before he ever came to the cross he knew loneliness, sorrow, exhaustion, disappointment, depression, temptation, desertion, and betrayal. On the cross he knew terrible pain—physical, emotional, and spiritual—and then (so it is said by doctors) he died of a broken heart.

Furthermore, Jesus not only *knows* your pain, *he feels it with you*. Again and again we read that Jesus was "moved with compassion." Some people seem to believe that because Jesus rose again and ascended to heaven he now does not feel our pain. Is he not moved with compassion any more? Of course he is. We read how Jesus wept in sympathy and grief. Does he not weep any more?

Of course he does. When Saul of Tarsus was murdering Christian men, women, and children, because of their faith in Christ, Jesus asked him, "Why are you persecuting me?" He didn't say "them". He said, "... me".

The Jesus you read of in the Gospels is the same Jesus who hears your heart-cry and stores up your tears. The Bible says, "Jesus Christ is the same yesterday and today and forever" (Hebrews 13:8). And one day he will wipe every tear from your eyes and mine, and we will never cry again.

Yes, in his life Jesus knew all these things that you and I have to contend with save one. He did not know the awful pain of guilt and shame because he never sinned. However intense the temptation—and it was more intense than any temptation you or I have ever undergone—he had the victory.

Until the cross. Then he was "made to *be sin*." Just think of that. This beautiful, sinless man suddenly knew the agony and the guilt and the shame of having committed every sin in the book. When you feel that indescribable shame for something you have done and you wish, oh how you wish, you could put back the clock and not have done that thing. If only you could erase it from your record. Then remember that God, for Christ's sake, *has* erased it and that God, for Christ's sake, *has* forgotten it. It is as if you had never done it. The Bible says:

> I, even I, am he who blots out your transgressions, for my own sake, and remembers your sins no more.
>
> (Isaiah 43:25)

But more: Christ knows what you are feeling because he once felt it too—only far, far worse. Even here he shares our pain.

Brother, sister, however dark your day, whatever your torments of the night, however intense your suffering, could you kneel at the cross and hear this anguished cry and still say, "Lord Jesus, you just don't know what I am going through and I don't think you care." I doubt it. I couldn't. I know he cares. I am certain of it.

141

The Certain Hope of his Presence

Jesus cried this cry of dereliction so that you and I need never cry it. He was forsaken of God so that you and I would never be. Not now, not ever. Once you trust in Christ and belong to him, you can never be forsaken. He always keeps his promises and he has said, "I will never leave you nor forsake you" (Hebrews 13:5 NKJV). Others may forsake you, Jesus never will.

Now there may be times when you might *feel* forsaken. We do not always sense the presence of the Lord. We walk by faith, not by sight. He has never promised that life will be easy. He calls upon disciples to carry a cross. Though we are his children, he sometimes (for his own purposes) allows us to suffer grief and pain. We must trust him even when we do not understand his ways. We must trust him in the dark as we do in the light. He does not explain all his ways. He is not obligated to do so.

When we cry, "My God, why?" we must come back again and again to the cross. When I do so I see the dear Son of God bleeding and dying and God-forsaken, and it was all *because he loved me*. I know that since my Savior went through all the pain of the cross for me he will not forsake me now.

> Is there a heart o'erbound by sorrow?
> Is there a life weighed down by care?
> Come to the cross—each burden bearing,
> All your anxiety—leave it there.
>
> All your anxiety, all your care,
> Bring to the mercy seat—leave it there;
> Never a burden He cannot bear,
> Never a friend like Jesus!
>
> —Edward Henry Joy

The Certain Hope of a Bright Tomorrow

You need to know that this cry is a quotation from the opening verse of Psalm 22. This Psalm has been called, "The Crucifixion

142

Psalm," because David was not only moved to write of his own experiences but, borne along by the Holy Spirit, he interwove remarkable and detailed prophecies concerning the suffering of the Christ. Consider these lines, for example:

> All who see me mock me; they hurl insults, shaking their heads: "He trusts in the Lord; let the Lord rescue him. Let him deliver him, since he delights in him." I am poured out like water, and all my bones are out of joint ... my tongue sticks to the roof of my mouth ... a band of evil men has encircled me, they have pierced my hands and my feet. They divide my garments among them and cast lots for my clothing.
>
> (Psalm 22:7, 8, 14-16, 18)

So close are these statements to what actually happened to the Lord Jesus on the cross that some have even accused him of deliberately manipulating events to make them fit the Psalm! One wonders how he is supposed to have talked the soldiers into gambling over his clothing.

The Lord Jesus lived these messianic scriptures. He declared, "We are going up to Jerusalem, and everything that is written by the prophets about the Son of Man will be fulfilled" (Luke 18:31). And after he had risen he gave his disciples a wonderful Bible study expounding these familiar passages. Jesus knew precisely what was going to happen to him in Jerusalem (that is why he shrank from it in the Garden of Gethsemane).

I believe the entirety of Psalm 22 was clearly in our Lord's mind as he hung on the cross. Just as some statements describe physical aspects of his agony such as the piercing of his hands and feet, and some emotional aspects such as the mockery and scorn, the opening cry of anguish perfectly suited his incomparably dreadful spiritual experience as our sin bearer.

But the Psalm is not a hopeless Psalm. Yes, it commences that way but the tone changes. It moves from desertion to deliverance, from pain to praise, from horror to hope. It speaks towards the end of the glory of God and of the triumph of the gospel. "All the ends of the earth will remember and turn to the Lord, and all the families of the nations will bow down before him" (Psalm 22:27).

Jesus knew how the Psalm ends, and he knew how the cross would end—in triumph. Soon he would shout a victory cry, "Te-telestai—It is accomplished!" As I have said, this cry of anguish, therefore, was not because he was perplexed not knowing why this was happening. His cry was not because he doubted the love or wisdom of his Father. It was the sheer, indescribable agony of soul which wrung this cry from his lips. So may we sometimes cry out in our pain, "My God, why?" Not because we are angry with God, or doubt his love, or demand explanations (wrong reasons), but *because pain hurts!*

Hebrews says:

> Let us fix our eyes on Jesus, the author and perfecter of our faith, who for the joy set before him endured the cross, scorning its shame, and sat down at the right hand of the throne of God. Consider him who endured such opposition from sinful men, so that you will not grow weary and lose heart.
>
> (Hebrews 12:2-3)

In other words, our Lord looked beyond his suffering to the joy which would soon be his. So must we. With God there will *always* be a bright tomorrow. Whatever awful thing you have to bear today, it will end. "Weeping may remain for a night, but rejoicing comes in the morning" (Psalm 30:5). Believe me, I know from my own experience.

Even though we have some affliction which God in his wisdom allows us to bear until the day we die, what is that compared with eternity? His grace will be our up-holding for each day, and when Jesus calls us home we shall enter heaven where love, joy, and peace abound, and where we will never hurt again.

When our Lord and Savior uttered the cry considered in this chapter, he had already promised to the man suffering and dying beside him, "Today you will be with me in Paradise." Jesus knew he would rise and reign.

Do you live on earth with an eye toward heaven? We should, you know. Jesus did. The Apostles did. The early Christians did. Our forefathers did. Today we are in danger of becoming totally obsessed with this world and this life and with ourselves. But the focus point of the Bible is the world to come and our future life in it. That is our destiny, our ultimate "bright tomorrow." We too will rise and reign—with Christ.

> Therefore we do not lose heart. Though outwardly we are wasting away, yet inwardly we are being renewed day by day. For our light and momentary troubles are achieving for us an eternal glory that far outweighs them all. So we fix our eyes not on what is seen, but on what is unseen. For what is seen is temporary, but what is unseen is eternal.
>
> (2 Corinthians 4:16-18)

> May I never boast except in the cross of our Lord Jesus Christ.
>
> (Galatians 6:14)

> Near the cross I'll watch and wait, hoping, trusting ever,
> Till I reach the golden strand just beyond the river.
> In the cross, in the cross be my glory ever,
> Till my raptured soul shall find rest, beyond the river.
>
> —Fanny J. Crosby

CHAPTER EIGHT

Cost

IT'S TOUGH BEING A FOLLOWER OF JESUS

Peter turned and saw that the disciple whom Jesus loved was
following them ...When Peter saw him he asked, "Lord, what
about him?" Jesus answered, "If I want him to remain alive until
I return, what is that to you? *You must follow me.*"

(John 21:20-22)

This chapter is about the cost of discipleship, and we will base it
upon some words which were uttered by the risen Lord Jesus
Christ to Simon Peter as part of a conversation which took place
early one morning on the shores of the Sea of Galilee, "You must
follow me." The story is told in John chapter 21.

When they had finished eating, Jesus said to Simon Peter, "Simon,
son of John, do you truly love me more than these?"
"Yes, Lord," he said, "you know that I love you."
Jesus said, "Feed my lambs."
Again Jesus said, "Simon, son of John, do you truly love me?"
He answered, "Yes, Lord, you know that I love you."
Jesus said, "Take care of my sheep."

The third time he said to him, "Simon, son of John, do you love
me?"
Peter was hurt because Jesus asked him the third time, "Do you
love me?" He said, "Lord, you know all things; you know that
I love you."
Jesus said, "Feed my sheep. I tell you the truth, when you were
younger you dressed yourself and went where you wanted; but
when you are old you will stretch out your hands, and someone
else will dress you and lead you where you do not want to go."
Jesus said this to indicate the kind of death by which Peter would
glorify God. Then he said to him, "Follow me!"
Peter turned and saw that the disciple whom Jesus loved was following them. (This was the one who had leaned back against Jesus
at the supper and had said, "Lord, who is going to betray you?")
When Peter saw him, he asked, "Lord, what about him?"
Jesus answered, "If I want him to remain alive until I return, what
is that to you? You must follow me."

(John 21:15-22)

Peter had three times declared his love for his Lord, and Jesus
three times reaffirmed Peter's apostolic ministry. Jesus then went
on to warn Peter that this love would one day cost him his life. He
would follow his Master to a cross. No doubt taken aback, Peter
looked over his shoulder and, seeing John nearby, he immediately
inquired of Jesus regarding the future destiny of his fellow apostle.
This brought forth the sharp reply which is our consideration in
this chapter. Taken alone it sounds almost a rebuke but, as we
will see, it was in fact a necessary reminder to Peter of the terms
of discipleship.

Every disciple—and every would-be disciple—will hear the
question put to Simon Peter, "Do you love me?" If we likewise
reply, "You know that I love you," then the Savior will say to us,
"Follow thou me" (KJV). We do well, therefore, to make ourselves
aware of what that call means.

1. FOLLOW ME—WITH UNQUESTIONING OBEDIENCE

The Lord Jesus had no sooner said to Simon Peter, "Follow
me," than Peter immediately queried it. "Lord, what about John?

What will happen to him?" It is as if he wants to question what Jesus had just said. But our Lord's command to him was not open to question. It was a "just do it" kind of command.

Now it is not always wrong to ask questions. Far from it. We learn by asking questions—and listening to answers. Questions which have to do with ascertaining the correct interpretation of the will of our Lord. Questions which seek to understand more accurately or deeply the truth revealed in God's Word. Our earnest desire with those sorts of questions is—or should be—obedience. There are, however, other kinds of questions which are really excuses to avoid obedience—or at least to postpone it.

My father used to say to me when I was a teenager and didn't want to do something, "Harry, why do you always want to question everything? Just do it!"

Is this not the trouble with many of us? We often want to question what our Lord has told us to do.

We acknowledge that:

Jesus is our *Master* and we are his servants (in fact the Bible usually uses the word "doulos", slave), and yet we are sometimes reluctant to obey.

Jesus is our *Sovereign* and we are his subjects, and yet we are slow to serve.

Jesus is our *Commander-in-chief* and we are soldiers in his army, and yet we do not always do what he commands.

We need to be reminded sometimes of all three of the above, but for now let us just consider the third. We have become soldiers of Jesus Christ and we are his to command. In the nineteenth-century, William Booth called the movement he founded, "The Salvation Army." It is a good term.

When I was eighteen years old, I was conscripted into the Royal Air Force. In England conscription was called, "National Service." There was no choice. You were drafted. I found that there were many ranks in the military, and a chain of command. Most people not only took commands from someone above them but had someone below them whom they could in turn command. Except for me!

I was just an "Airman Class II," the lowest of the low, the bottom of the pile. I did not command anybody.

Now if the sergeant had said to me, "Kilbride, pick up that pack."

And I had said, "Well that is an interesting request, Sergeant. I would like to discuss this with you. I have a question. I was just wondering if Smith here is going to pick up any packs."

If I had said any of that I would not be here to write this book! You know, men disappeared off the face of the earth who questioned the sergeant's command! You were trained from the beginning that, if he says do it, you do it. You just do it.

But we Christians say, "Yes, Lord Jesus. You are my Lord, my King, my Commander. I hear your call, 'Follow me.' Well, I will certainly try. However, I have a question—or two, or three. Stewardship? Possessions? Giving? Relationships? Not storing up treasure on earth? Praying every day? Evangelizing the lost? Caring for the poor? Forgiving that one who wronged me? Well, Lord, you know that I love you, but I must think a bit more about these commands. They are a bit—um—tough. Maybe tomorrow."

How does Jesus know that we mean it when we tell him that we love him? Lots of people tell people they love them but it does not mean anything. How do we give substance to our declaration? Answer: by obeying his commands. Jesus said this:

> If you love me, you will obey what I command ... Whoever has my commands and obeys them, he is the one who loves me. He who loves me will be loved by my Father ... If anyone loves me, he will obey my teaching.
>
> (John 14:15, 21, 23)

The inescapable conclusion we must draw from these words of our Lord is that true love for him leads to obedience. Obedience is therefore both the fruit of our love for him and the evidence that our discipleship-love is real.

These words also teach us that love is the *motive* Jesus wants in his disciple's obedience. There can be obedience through fear, such as the obedience I gave to my sergeant. Or obedience through moral duty, such as that I give to traffic laws—well most of the time! But the best obedience is motivated by love, and *that* is what our Lord speaks of in John, chapter 14, and in his challenge to Peter. Love, then, is the motive for a disciple's obedience and *the power of it*. The more love we have for Christ the more eagerly we will want to please him in all things.

Disciple of Jesus, do you truly love him? Then follow him—and follow him with unquestioning obedience.

2. Follow Me—AND ACCEPT THE CROSS

Jesus warned Peter, "... When you are old you will stretch out your hands, and someone else will dress you and lead you where you do not want to go." Comments John, "Jesus said this to indicate the kind of death by which Peter would glorify God. Then he said to him, 'Follow me!'" (John 21:18-19). Early documents tell us that Peter died by crucifixion in Rome during the persecution of Emperor Nero.

Mercifully the Lord spares most of us from knowing when or how we will die. However, the Lord Jesus calls all his disciples to sacrifice in one way or another. That is why we talk about laying our lives on the altar. Salvation is free, but discipleship costs everything. Nothing, it seems to me, is so misleading as when preachers give new converts the impression that it is *easy* to follow Jesus, and that to live the life of a disciple of Jesus is just a "bed of roses." As I have noted in previous chapters, that is the very opposite of what Jesus taught.

Jesus said, "In this world you will have trouble..." (John 16:33), and, "If anyone would come after me, he must deny himself and take up his cross daily and follow me" (Luke 9:23). When Jesus speaks of disciples being called to bear a cross, he is not speaking of the ordinary trials of life—Shakespeare's, "the heartache and the thousand natural shocks that flesh is heir to." He is speaking of something which the disciple is called upon to voluntarily *take up*—something costly, something painful, something for which the only appropriate metaphor is the awful cruelty of death on a cross.

Some other words of Jesus are, perhaps, even more astonishing. Consider them:

> Large crowds were traveling with Jesus, and turning to them he said: "If anyone comes to me and does not hate his father and mother, his wife and children, his brothers and sisters—yes, even his own life—he cannot be my disciple. And anyone who does not carry his cross and follow me cannot be my disciple. Suppose one of you wants to build a tower. Will he not first sit down and estimate the cost?"
>
> (Luke 14:25-28)

> Do not suppose that I have come to bring peace to the earth. I did not come to bring peace, but a sword. For I have come to turn "a man against his father, a daughter against her mother, a daughter-in-law against her mother-in-law—a man's enemies will be the members of his own household."
>
> (Matthew 10:34-36)

We do not hear much of these sayings nowadays do we? Perhaps we don't want to. Jesus is calling would-be disciples to stop, think, and count the cost. Discipleship will be tough and involve sacrifice. Would we not today more likely be trying to persuade as many people in the crowd as possible to "make a decision for Christ" by making it as painless and alluring as possible, in some cases even promising "heaven now"—health, wealth, and a trouble-free life? To inflate our statistics and fill our churches, we frequently offer a *cost*-less, *cross*-less and even *mind*-less discipleship. Shame on us! That was not the way of our Lord Jesus.

Reading again our Lord's words you may be saying, "I am shocked. I thought we were supposed to love people. I thought we were supposed to love our family. What does Jesus mean by hate our father and our mother and so forth?" I agree it is a hard saying. Many of our Lord's words were "hard sayings." We conveniently avoid them if we can. This one was what we call a Hebraism. It was a way of speaking in Jesus' time. When faced with painful choices, when you have to choose one thing rather than another, it may seem as if you hate the one that comes second. In reality you simply choose to love one *more*. Of course Jesus not only taught us to love our families but also our neighbors, and even our enemies. Nevertheless if we put the Lord Jesus *first*—even above dearly loved family—it may seem (at least to them) that we hate them.

Whether you understand that strange saying or not, let me tell you it frequently comes true. People give their lives to Jesus Christ and they go back to their unsaved family and their family turns against them. It may be one member of the family, it may be more than one, but they are told, "You brought division in this house." They say, "You are not like you used to be. You are different. Something has happened to you." They say, "You hate us. You are 'holier than thou.' You look down upon us."

And the Christian daughter or son says, "Oh, I do not hate you, Mom and Dad. Brothers and sisters, I do not hate you. I love you more than I ever loved you, but I love Jesus first, and I cannot do what you want me to do. Yes, I *am* a different person."

For example, when a Jewish person comes to believe in Jesus as the Messiah, the hostility of the uncomprehending family can sometimes be very severe. The family may even disown them. When a Muslim person converts to Christ it can cost him, or her, their lives. That is strict Islamic teaching. Conversion carries the death penalty.

A Story of Sacrifice

Some years ago I visited Sicily, where some Italian friends minister the Gospel and have a Gospel radio station. If you know your geography you will remember that Italy is shaped like a long boot kicking a football. The "football" is the beautiful island of Sicily. Five million people live in Sicily, which unfortunately is most famous, not for its spectacular mountain scenery, rugged coastline, ancient Greek temples, or vineyards and olive-groves, but for spawning the Mafia.

In the hills above Ribera, up a winding mountain road, in the village of Lucca, I met a lady, long widowed, and her daughter.

How did she become widowed, this dear woman who had a little church that met in her house?

Before the Second World War her husband was a tailor traveling from village to village plying his craft. But he was a very unhappy man. He had been pursuing happiness but he had never found it; not in his family, not in his work, and not in his religion. He was a very devout Roman Catholic and he burned a candle to St. Anthony every day but it brought him no satisfaction.

"Is this all there is to life?" he asked himself.

One day he forgot to snuff out the candle and it burned on and on and on, until the little image of St. Anthony became defaced. In fact it melted. At first he was dismayed, but then he reflected on its symbolic significance. What power could this image have if it melted before a forgotten candle? He went to see his priest.

The priest said to him, "Son, do you want to know God personally?"

"Yes, father," he said, "I want to know the living God more than anything in the world. Is it really possible to know God?"

Replied the priest, "Go down into Ribera, there is a group of people who meet in a home. They meet to study the Bible, to sing and to pray. I believe they truly know God."

So he went to see if this thing could be true, and he found it was so. This group of born-again believers pointed him to the Savior. He heard the gospel message, how God is to be known through Jesus Christ who came into the world to show us God, and to bring us to God. The tailor knelt at the cross and gave his heart and life to Jesus Christ who is the way, the truth, and the life.

"Do you love me?" the Risen Savior asked him.

"You know that I love you, Lord Jesus."

And Jesus replied, "Follow me."

The tailor owned an orchard and every year he would be forced to pay to the Mafia money for 'protection' of his orchard. They came to him as usual at the beginning of the year and demanded money.

He said, "I cannot give you money anymore. I have found the Lord and I trust in him for protection."

The following day he found every one of his precious fruit trees cut to the ground.

Undeterred, he went into the villages and began to tell people of Jesus and to share his newfound faith. Though it was widely known what his discipleship had cost him, others were converted including his wife and daughter. Mussolini had him arrested and put into a concentration camp on the mainland of Italy. In conditions of severe deprivation he worked and languished through the years of the war. He arrived home in 1945 a very sick man. Two years later he died, aged thirty-seven.

Why did the sovereign Lord allow all this and take him to heaven so young? I do not know. I do know this, however, that Jesus said, "I tell you the truth, unless a kernel of wheat falls to the ground and dies, it remains only a single seed. But if it dies, it produces many seeds" (John 12:24). I also know that from the rooftop of the house where he lived, and where the widow and her daughter still were living, there is an antenna that picks up a signal from the Gospel radio station in Ribera and wings it out hundreds of miles across the island. I know that many people have found the Savior through that radio station and its mountain village extension. I do not understand the link between those two things, but I think we may find that somehow there is one. He laid down his life, and Jesus made it fruitful.

Simon Peter was to face a cross. Perhaps that is what he flinched from in the courtyard of the High Priest when he denied his Lord. He was brave when his blood was hot. He unwisely boasted that though his fellow disciples might deny their Lord, he would never do so. In Gethsemane's garden he was prepared to fight the entire Roman army and die in action. Bravo!

But the test did not come that way. It came through the questions and taunts of a girl. Satan often attacks us when and where we least expect it. Disguised and very subtle, he exploits our weakness. A tough, middle-aged, Galilean fisherman would stand up and fight another man anytime but did not want to appear to have backed a loser when questioned by a girl, especially in front of some other fellows warming themselves around a fire. Besides this, Jesus was now under arrest. An admission of association with Jesus might result in his own arrest and execution.

I do not know what your test will be, or your cross. It might be in your family but it might be in your career. Perhaps you will be asked to compromise your Christian principles and deny your Lord. If you refuse to do so, your cross could be in being passed up for promotion. Imagine trying to get on in the world of science-teaching if you don't believe in Darwinian evolution. What is it like for some nurses who refuse to assist in abortions? Your cross may be no worse(?) than the fact that, though your colleagues like you and admire you because as a Christian you are truthful, cheerful, loyal and diligent, yet they keep you at arms length because you are—well—different. You are "religious;" one of those strange "born-again" types. Best to be avoided! You may be branded a "right-wing fundamentalist" and dismissed either as an oddity, a menace to a libertarian society, or both.

The Apostle Paul said, "Present your bodies a *living sacrifice*." We naturally fear to die—especially a violent death—but it may sometimes be harder to *live* for Christ than to *die* for him.

Can we evade the cross? Sometimes we can. Since it is something we are called upon to "take up" we may refuse it. Peter refused to accept the cross when he denied he ever knew Jesus and did so with oaths and curses. But he bitterly regretted his choice.

The paradox is this: no one is as miserable as the true disciple of Jesus who has refused the cross. In the denial or compromise to avoid the pain, the disciple only finds that the pain of regret and shame is far worse. Praise God there is for all, as for Peter, forgiveness, cleansing, restoration, and another opportunity to be faithful.

Christian disciples, do you love Jesus? Will you accept the cross?

3. FOLLOW ME—AND DON'T COMPARE

Lordship is sovereign and it is individual. He is Lord over *me*. I have given my heart to him. I have bent the knee to him. I am his servant, his subject, and his soldier. He can do with me, therefore, whatever he wants. He can also do with Michael, and Andrew, and Sarah, and Emily whatever he wants. What he appoints for others may not be the same as for me. *I must not compare my lot with that of someone else or I may be in trouble.*

Now there are, of course, some things he offers the same to all. All who come to him receive the forgiveness of all their sins, his daily presence through the indwelling Holy Spirit, and a future inheritance in heaven. There are other ways, however, in which we are treated differently. To one he appoints riches, and to another hardship. To one he grants good health, but another is apportioned sickness. One he calls to be married, another he calls to be single. To one he gives 20/20 vision, but another may be permitted to be blind.

May I remind you again that in Hebrews chapter 11, in the great gallery of heroes of faith, we come in verse 32 to these words,

> And what more shall I say? I do not have time to tell about Gideon, Barak, Samson, Jephthah, David, Samuel and the prophets, who through faith conquered kingdoms, administered justice, and gained what was promised; who shut the mouths of lions, quenched the fury of the flames, and escaped the edge of the sword; whose weakness was turned to strength; and who became powerful in battle and routed foreign armies. Women received back their dead, raised to life again....
>
> (Hebrews 11:32-35)

Is *that* the life of faith where lions cannot touch you and flames cannot burn you? Well, it clearly was for those mentioned above. However, go on in Hebrews 11 from verse 35:

> Others were tortured and refused to be released, so that they might gain a better resurrection. Some faced jeers and flogging, while still others were chained and put in prison. They were stoned; they were sawed in two; they were put to death by the sword. They went about in sheepskins and goatskins, destitute, persecuted, and mistreated—the world was not worthy of them. They wandered in deserts and mountains, and in caves and holes in the ground. These were all commended for their faith, yet none

of them received what had been promised. God had planned
something better....

(Hebrews 11:35-40)

What if these 'others' had said, "Well, you delivered Daniel,
why are you not doing the same for me?" They would have lost
their joy and their peace. Comparisons are not only odious they
are fatal to victorious discipleship. The Lord Jesus is saying to us,
"Look, when you gave me your heart you gave me *your* heart, *your*
life. Do not compare yourself with someone else."

I was for three years Field Director of a Missionary Society. I
remember once asking one of our workers if he could manage on
the allowance we sent him.

"Yes," he replied, "we can manage, but if I thought someone else
was getting more—well, that would be hard to take, I must say!"

At least he was honest. Are not many of us inclined to think in
a similar way? We would be satisfied except that we have looked
over our shoulders and observed someone whom we think has a
better deal. Then we complain. Why should he have that car and
not me? Why should she get that job (or that child, or that house,
or that trip) and not me? Why has that tragedy happened to me
when nothing bad seems to happen to him? Jesus said to Peter
regarding John, "If I want him to remain alive until I return, what
is that to you? You must follow me."

Obviously John did not remain alive until the return of Christ.
Neither did he have it easy. Though he lived to a ripe old age, he
did so as an exiled prisoner on the island of Patmos, cutting rocks
in the blistering sun. Jesus could have explained that to Peter in
answer to his question. Jesus might have said, "Oh, John will have
it tough too. His destiny will not be quite the same as yours but it
will be just as costly. Peter, don't think that John will have an easier
time." But that was not the point. The destiny of John was Jesus'
business not Peter's. "Mind your own business," Jesus is saying,
"*You* must follow me." The personal pronoun is very emphatic in
the Greek.

Perhaps this is the hardest aspect of discipleship—to be *content* with whatever the Master has appointed for us. Even Paul had to learn the secret (Philippians 4:10-13). Envy and jealousy are hard dragons to kill. I read one famous preacher's testimony in which he said that he did not think he had a jealous bone in his body until he was preaching in a certain city, and he heard that another preacher was having a series of meetings in a church across town and was drawing bigger crowds. Then—and only then—did the dormant green-headed monster rise up and seek to devour him.

By the way, Jesus himself was single, was poor, was very lonely, was usually misunderstood—even by his own family—was betrayed, was tortured, died young, and died very cruelly. He had large crowds but few disciples, and even they deserted him in his hour of need. He does not ask anyone to follow except along a pathway he himself has trod.

Christian disciple, do you love Jesus? Then follow him and *don't compare.*

4. Follow Me—AND FULFIL YOUR MINISTRY

When Simon Peter affirmed his love for the Savior, Jesus immediately gave him his ministry.

"Feed my lambs," v15.
"Take care of my sheep," v 16.
"Feed my sheep," v17.

Peter was thus reappointed to be a leader, a pastor, and a preacher. We know from a study of the Acts of the Apostles that Peter fulfilled that ministry, and also became an inspired writer of God's Word in the form of two New Testament letters.

A call to discipleship always involves a call to ministry. We are saved to serve. Obviously we are not all called and appointed to be pastors and teachers, but each one of us has our appointed sphere of service. (See Ephesians 4:9-13.) Disciple, are you serving?

Let us be clear about one thing; our Christian service is not confined to that which we do in church. Our daily work, appointed of the Lord and done as 'unto him', is also service for Christ.

> Slaves, obey your earthly masters in everything; and do it, not only when their eye is on you and to win their favor, but with sincerity of heart and reverence for the Lord. Whatever you do, work at it with all your heart, as working for the Lord, not for men, since you know that you will receive an inheritance from the Lord as a reward. It is the Lord Christ you are serving.
>
> (Colossians 3:22-24)

When our Lord Jesus worked at his books as a boy, and at his bench as a man, he was doing the will of God his Father just as much as when he left the carpenter's shop to preach and to heal. A mother tending and teaching her children is as busy as anyone can be and serves her Savior therein. Nevertheless, few of us can legitimately claim to have no time at all that can also be used in one of the ministries of our local church.

No disciple is too *old* to serve. Those aged saints confined to home—or even to bed—may breathe a petition and thus exercise their most powerful and fruitful ministry when they may least think so.

No disciple is too *young* to serve.

You may think that you are too *sinful* to serve. Wrong—unless you are an unrepentant sinner, willfully continuing in your sin. We are all sinners—sinners saved by grace. The only sinners disqualified from Christian service are unrepentant ones. The moment you come to Jesus confessing your sin trusting in him, and him alone, to save you by his blood shed on the cross, your sins are blotted out and are gone for ever. When Simon Peter failed it was not his salvation that was in jeopardy—for all his sins were covered by the cross—but his unclouded fellowship with his Lord.

Three times he had denied his Lord. So, three times Jesus asked him, "Do you love me?" and thereby offered him the opportunity to three times reaffirm his love. It was then that Jesus gave Peter his commission—three times.

There is something else here—and it is in some respects the main message of the entire story. Peter may have imagined that he had forfeited the right to fulfill the ministry of an apostle because he had sinned *as a disciple—even as an apostle.* To be forgiven is one thing, but to be restored to church leadership and a public ministry of teaching and preaching is quite another. After all, Peter had let his Lord down, sinned grievously, and betrayed his high calling. Could anything be much worse than what Peter did? To have spent three remarkable years with Jesus as one of the Twelve, and been in the privileged trio to witness Jesus' transfiguration, his agony in Gethsemane, and other intimate events, only to then deny that he had ever known him—why that must rank high on any list of sins, don't you think? And poor Peter did this with foul profanity, calling down curses upon those who accused him of being Jesus' friend.

Yes: Peter had repented with bitter tears and his Lord had met with him privately to assure him—I believe—of complete forgiveness. (See Luke 24:34, 1 Corinthians 15:5.) Nevertheless, it would not be surprising if Peter thought his days of apostleship were over.

The Lord Jesus thought otherwise. This encounter was about restoration to ministry. My New International Version rightly gives this story the heading, "Jesus Reinstates Peter."

Maybe there is someone reading this chapter who has also let the Lord down; maybe in the way Peter did, or maybe in some other way. Maybe your sin was private, known only to God, and is your 'guilty secret.' Or maybe your sin was public and known to many. If the latter, you can be sure that some of your fellow Christians will tell you that you can never serve again. And if they don't, Satan will. It was Satan who arranged the temptation of Peter in the courtyard of the High Priest. Jesus said so (Luke 22:31-32). And there was nothing Satan would like more now than to make sure that Peter was disabled forever.

Peter couldn't say, "The devil made me do it"—and neither can we. Satan can never *make* anyone sin. We willfully do it. The responsibility is our own. That does not mean, however, that Satan the master strategist does not devilishly go after those whom he fears the most and lays some traps.

My brother or sister: Don't listen to the devil. If you listened to him once, don't listen to him now. In other words, if Satan won a battle don't let him win the war.

Wrote St. Benedict:

I am wounded but I am not slain
I will lie me down and bleed awhile.
Then rise and fight again.

Praise God! That is the message of this story. Those whom the Lord forgives he also restores. He binds up the brokenhearted, he recycles the discarded, and he heals (not shoots) the wounded warrior. Don't bleed for long.

Some have suggested that this restoration of Peter was "an exception." No: quite the contrary. This is the consistent message throughout the Bible. We not only have the example of Simon Peter, but there are many others. Had I the space I could tell of Abraham, of Moses, of David, and many more, sinners all who were treated with the same forgiving and *restoring* love.

Little wonder God says "'For my thoughts are not your thoughts, neither are your ways my ways,' declares the Lord" (Isaiah 55:8). Let me tell you something: God is indeed different from men. His ways are not our ways. *He is far, far kinder.* He is full of understanding, of compassion, and of love.

Many years ago I was a High School teacher. Sometimes a boy or a girl would spoil their work with blots and stains and erasures. They had blotted their copybook. Shamefaced and upset they would bring it to show me.

Sometimes I would ask, "Would you like me to tear out that page? Then you can start over with a clean one."

That offer was never declined, I can tell you.

I did that because that is what my Lord had done for me. He is the God of the clean page. Friend: have you "blotted your copy-book?" Well, have you returned to the loving arms of Christ? Then that page is gone. I said *gone. Gone forever*!!! Don't walk around still carrying the burden of guilt for that which God has blotted out. You may have secrets from the past but no *guilty* ones. Not so far as the Lord is concerned. They are shredded. Today is a *clean page.*

Guess who Jesus chose to be the preacher, a few weeks later, on the Day of Pentecost, the Inauguration Day of the Church?

Simon Peter.

Our Own Memories

Someone may ask me, "Harry, if the Lord forgets our sins, why can we not forget our own sins?"

Answers:

- so that we will not sin again;
- so that we will magnify God's grace;
- so that we will, if possible, keep well away from the kind of situations which led to our defeat;
- so that we might remain humble, slow to condemn others, and swift to forgive.

5. FOLLOW ME—YOU HAVE A GLORIOUS FUTURE

Who is this man who calls us to follow him unconditionally, even though it means a cross?

Why should we obey his costly call and follow him?

Because he is the King of Kings and Lord of Lords

Let us notice again the words Jesus said to Peter in answer to his question concerning John. "If I want him to remain alive until I return..." Again I like the way it is put in the old version "If I will that he tarry till I come..." (KJV). "*If I will...*" The Lord Jesus Christ is hereby declaring that he will determine the future destiny of both Peter and John.

- Not Caiaphas—gloating in the house of the High Priest because he thought he had rid himself of a dangerous upstart;

- not Pontius Pilate—feasting in the Governor's Mansion because he thought he had skillfully evaded a tricky political situation;
- not paranoid King Herod—partying in his palace because he imagined that yet another threat to his throne had been removed;
- not the Emperor in far off Rome—who imagined he ruled the world;
- not the mob—who howled for Jesus' blood;
- none of these—nor any others.

Jesus, and Jesus alone, holds the destiny of Peter and John in the hollow of his hand—and, for that matter, the destiny of Caiaphas, Pilate, Herod, Nero, and every other man, woman, and child who has ever lived, or ever will live.

Before he ascended to heaven, Jesus assured his assembled disciples, "All authority in heaven and on earth has been given to me." Not merely some authority, you will notice, but *all*; not only in heaven, but on *earth*. Not only on some future earth in some future age, but on *this* earth in *this* age. If not, he could not have said, "Therefore go and make disciples of all nations" (Matthew 28:18-19).

An aged John, enslaved on the island of Patmos, had a vision of the risen and reigning Lord Jesus. He wrote about it in the Book of Revelation.

> When I saw him, I fell at his feet as though dead. Then he placed his right hand on me and said: "Do not be afraid. I am the First and the Last. I am the Living One; I was dead, and behold I am alive for ever and for ever! And I hold the keys of death and Hades."
>
> (Revelation 1:17-18)

Little wonder that John describes Jesus as, "King of Kings and Lord of Lords," and, "… the ruler of the kings of the earth" (Revelation 19:16; 1:5).

Oh, what a comfort it is to me when I lie down to sleep at night and rise to a new day to know that I belong to the One who alone determines what befalls me. Unless the Lord returns first, one day I will die. I should not be afraid because that cannot happen until he has appointed it. Not a second sooner or later. When my work on earth is done he will call me home. In Acts, chapter 12, we read what happened the next time Peter was called upon to suffer for Jesus' sake. Arrested and imprisoned, the night before his expected execution Peter slept like a baby.

Will we not, therefore, gladly obey the call of Jesus, the Sovereign Lord, to follow him and trust him, no matter what in his wise providence he appoints for us?

Why should we follow him?

Because he is the One who Loves us Like no Other

He is the King with nail-pierced hands. As Peter watched the risen Savior prepare that breakfast, he could not help but notice the scarred hands. As Jesus walked beside him while Peter declared his love, Peter would surely see the prints of the nails on his sandaled feet. The Lord Jesus will be the only one in heaven with a wounded body. They are glorified wounds. They are there so that we will never forget his love, never forget his sacrifice, and never forget the cross.

If we ever doubt his love we must come back to the cross again and again. We must constantly dwell beneath its shadow. One reason why the Lord left us the ordinance of the Lord's Supper was to remind us of the cross.

Do you ever doubt his love? He loves you enough that he died for you. And if he did that, then will he not watch over you? He cares about every problem you face, every moment you live, every tear you shed.

Why should we follow him?

Because His Kingdom is Glorious and has no End

What is your purpose in life? Do you have one?

George Bernard Shaw, the famous playwright wrote, "This is the true joy of life, the being used for a purpose recognized by yourself as a mighty one; the being thoroughly worn out before you are thrown on the scrap heap; the being a force of nature instead of a feverish selfish little clod of ailments and grievances complaining that the world will not devote itself to making you happy." I find that a challenge coming from a man who was not a Christian.

The question is, what "purpose recognized by myself as a mighty one" shall I choose? Will it be political, or social, or philanthropic? What mighty purpose can compare with following and serving the Lord Jesus Christ, the King of Kings, who, when he determines that our purpose on earth is complete does not throw us "on the scrap heap", but takes us to heaven to await the glorious consummation of his kingdom?

Nothing we do in Christ's name will ever be consigned to a scrap heap. Even the smallest action has eternal significance and reaps an eternal reward. Whatever we are called upon to sacrifice for Jesus is nothing but an investment in our future glory. That is why our Lord told us not to store up treasure on earth but send it on ahead.

Wrote missionary martyr Jim Eliot, "He is no fool who gives what he cannot keep to gain what he cannot lose."

6. Follow Me—AND KEEP YOUR EYES ON JESUS

Our text says, "Peter *turned*." Our Lord Jesus Christ had just said to Peter, "Follow me," and lo and behold, he immediately took his eyes away from Jesus to look elsewhere. That was seemingly not only a problem for Simon Peter but it is for so many of us also. We must not turn our gaze from Christ or else when the going gets tough, or in the moment of temptation we may fail. Turning is fateful to faithful discipleship.

We must not turn *back*

When following the Lord becomes costly and difficult, some disciples are tempted to turn away from Jesus and look back to their pre-conversion days. Instead of recalling the wastefulness, the futility, the guilt, and the emptiness, they put on tinted glasses and recall the easy times. Even the Israelites forgot how they groaned under the lashes of their cruel Egyptian slave masters and began to look longingly back towards Egypt (Numbers 11:4-5).

The road of discipleship may sometimes be rough and steep and lonely, but it leads to heaven. The broad road is well-traveled but it leads to destruction. Oh disciple, don't turn back! The old road will not be as easy and attractive as you might think.

> She set a rose to blossom in her hair,
> The day faith died.
> "Now glad," she said, "and free at last, I go,
> And life is wide."
> But through long nights she stared into the dark,
> And knew she lied.
>
> —Fannie Heaslip Lea

Some look back in a different way. They look back to incidents of hurt and pain and become paralyzed with bitterness or regret. They become what Shaw so colorfully described as, "a feverish selfish little clod of ailments and grievances complaining that the world will not devote itself to making [them] happy." How terrible when such a person professes to be a follower of Jesus Christ. It could never describe you, could it?

It may not be something in the past done *to* us which captures our gaze but something done *by* us. We have considered why our Lord allows us some memory of our sins. I must tell you that he never wants us to focus upon them or dwell upon them. As we have emphasized, they were paid for by Christ on the cross. They have been expunged from God's record book. If Peter had stayed wallowing in self pity for the mistakes of yesterday, he would never have become the great leader of the apostolic church.

Wrote Paul, "Forgetting what is behind and straining towards what is ahead, I press on toward the goal to win the prize for which God has called me heavenward in Christ Jesus" (Philippians 3:13,14). Discipleship is like running a race. It is not a sprint. It is more like a marathon. If we stumble we must get up and go on. The prize is not for who comes first but for all who finish.

We must not even turn *aside*

If we turn our gaze away from Christ and look at our circumstances—as Peter once did when he looked at the waves—we too will sink.

If we turn our gaze away from Christ and listen to the unbelievers—as Peter once did—we may deny him.

If we look over our shoulder at a fellow believer, we might hesitate, or compare.

> Therefore, holy brothers, who share in the heavenly calling, fix your thoughts on Jesus.
>
> (Hebrews 3:1)

> Let us fix our eyes on Jesus, the author and perfecter of our faith.
>
> (Hebrews 12:1)

IN CONCLUSION

The Lord Jesus never deceived anyone. "Follow thou me," he calls; and promises us a cross to carry, an enemy to fight, a task to fulfill, a cause to advance, a race to complete, and a crown to win. Is that it? Anything else? Oh yes. Our Lord also promises:

> *a peace* which the world can never give;
> *a joy* which cannot be quenched;
> *a freedom* which cannot be constrained;
> *a happiness* which does not depend upon happenings; and
> *an abundant life* in his kingdom.

There, tears will be wiped away, and suffering, sin, and death will be no more. There, righteousness, beauty, love, and glory will reign for ever. We will reign with him in a new heaven and a new earth. I can hardly wait.

I was about to write, "These are priceless blessings", but of course they are not priceless. The Son of God came from heaven and went to the cross, that he might pay the greatest price, the only price, even his own blood.

But if we would have the blessings of being a disciple of Jesus we must accept the terms. For these few short years of our pilgrimage we must carry the cross, wage the war, fulfill the task, advance the cause, run the race, and strive for the crown.

If we share his sufferings *now*, we will share his glory *then*; if we accept the *cross* today, we will wear the *crown* tomorrow.

Satan will tempt us to take the easy way. He came to our Lord himself and showed him all the kingdoms of the world and said, "All this I will give you if you will bow down and worship me" (Matthew 4:9).

He is still trying the same strategy. "Do not go God's way. It is too costly. It is the way of self-denial and a cross. All these things will I give you…"

What things? Oh, a few trinkets.

Jesus asked him, "Do you love me?"
"Lord you know all things; you know that I love you."
"… Follow me … You must follow me."

I have decided to follow Jesus,
No turning back.

The world behind me, the Cross before me,
No turning back.

Tho' none go with me, I still will follow,
No turning back.

Will you decide now to follow Jesus?
No turning back.

Questions for Further Discussion

CHAPTER 1: TRAGEDY

1. Some people assume that when bad things happen to a person
    God must be punishing them for some sin they have commit-
    ted. What is wrong with this conclusion?
    Does God *ever* punish a sinner in this life by sending (or per-
    mitting) some hardship or suffering?

2. On page 6 it states, "Though I have no statistics to prove it I
    have a hunch that Christians suffer as many disasters as non-
    Christians." Do you agree? Or do you think Christians experi-
    ence fewer hardships?

3. In light of all the suffering in this world, on what evidence do
    Christians still assert that God is love?

4. When faced with tragedy what requests are appropriate for us
    to make as we approach God in prayer?

5. Romans 8:28 states, "And we know that in all things God works for the good of those who love him, who have been called according to his purpose." What "good" may God bring from an evil tragedy such as the murder of Mary Kilbride?

CHAPTER 2: HARDSHIP

1. Suggest some wrong conclusions a Christian may draw when hardship comes along.

2. Read again Romans 8:18-29. Review the points drawn out in the chapter from this rich and revealing passage.

3. Briefly share with your group any example from your own experience when you felt your "brook had dried up." How did the Lord provide for you after that?

CHAPTER 3: DEPRESSION I

1. Do you think that depression is always a sin? If not, why not?

2. Can you remember—after reading this chapter—which men of God in the Bible also experienced times of depression? Do you think Jesus was ever depressed? What about in the Garden of Gethsemane?

3. Why does God allow his precious servants to pass through times of depression?

4. Do you agree that "a grudge against life is a grudge against God?"

5. When might depression be holy?

CHAPTER 4: DEPRESSION II

1. What do you understand by the word "grace"? The author tells a story from his childhood of when he received grace from an uncle. Does any member of the group recall a similar experience in their own life which they can share briefly?

2. It says of Jesus, "A bruised reed he will not break, and a smoldering wick he will not snuff out." What does it mean? Can you give modern day illustrations of how that might be true?

3. The author asks, "...do you remember such practical angels during some dark period of your life?" If you do, share it with your group.

4. If you are depressed because you are lonely what steps, if any, can you take to try to remedy that? Do you agree that churches can be lonely places for a stranger? Why is this? What should be done about it?

5. Why should a Christian never despair?

CHAPTER 5: DEPRESSION III

1. In seeking God what might be the value of visiting a special place, away from your normal surroundings? Has anyone in the group experienced such a special place?

2. The chapter states that we often put on a mask before other people, but we should not do so with God. In what ways do

we disguise our true feelings and is it right to do this? When is it necessary and when would it be better to be open and honest?

3. The author says, "It seems to me that many churches, as well as many Christians, need a fresh encounter with the majestic holiness of God. We have become too trivial". Do you agree? If so, suggest examples.

4. Many Christians can testify that they have heard the gentle whisper of the Lord calling their name. What do they mean? Do you think it was a voice that could be recorded? If it was an inward impression, how could they be sure it was the Lord? Could such claims be dangerous—even blasphemous?

5. Learning from Elijah's experience, why should we always trust God for our future?

CHAPTER 6: DOUBT

1. Is it a sin to have doubts?

2. Who do you think are the prime targets in Satan's warfare? It pays to know the enemy and his tactics. How do you think Satan might attack you?

3. Jesus and John appear to have been different in lifestyle. What lessons can we draw from this? Are all lifestyles legitimate? Should we publicly or privately criticize the lifestyles of others?

4. Consider some *wrong* places to look for answers to doubts. Where does the author say is the place to look? What is unique

about Jesus' message of salvation? Why is it difficult to explain away Jesus' healing miracles as psychosomatic (mind over body)?

5. On what evidence would you suggest that Jesus was not (i) "mad" or (ii) "bad"? What convinces you that Jesus is God the Son, and the true Messiah?

CHAPTER 7: ANGUISH

1. The author states that though he is afraid of pain, he is not afraid to die. Why not?

2. How would *you* explain the cross to someone who asks you, "Why did Jesus die?"

3. Sometimes when loved ones are dying they say things that are distressing to those caring for them. Why is this, and how should we handle it?

4. God is holy and is repulsed by sin. God is just and must punish sin. Are there any circumstances where we reflect the same reactions?

5. What "good works" do some people imagine will get them a place in heaven? Why is this a false hope?

6. Why does the author hear hope in such an anguished cry as this?

CHAPTER 8: COST

1. Do you think that the reply of Jesus to Peter's question (John 21:20-22) was a rebuke? If so, why was it necessary?

2. How would you understand the seemingly hard words of Jesus recorded in Luke 14:25-28 and Matthew 10:34-36? Do you know of any examples where following Christ has brought family division?

3. Share practical examples of the cost of discipleship in a place of work. Do some Christians bring unnecessary approbation upon themselves by their behavior?

4. The author writes, "Turning is fateful for faithful discipleship." To what, to where, and to whom might we be tempted to turn?

5. As well as a cross to carry, what blessings does the Lord Jesus promise to all who will follow him?

To order additional copies of

When the Road is

ROUGH AND STEEP

Have your credit card ready and call:

1-877-421-READ (7323)

or please visit our web site at
www.pleasantword.com

Also available at:
www.amazon.com
and
www.barnesandnoble.com

Printed in the United States
48041LVS00006B/1-51